Ravishing Raves
for
Love's Reckless Rash:

"*Love's Reckless Rash* does for the gothic romance what *The Hitchhiker's Guide to the Galaxy* did for science fiction.... Hilarious."

—*Playboy*

"Moft amufing..."

—Alfred Gingold
Author of *Items from Our Catalog*

"*Love's Reckless Rash* is a riot, an affectionate and very witty spoof.... Definitely a must for those who like laughter and love."

—Vanessa Royall
Author of *Flames of Desire*

"I cackled with mirth through *Love's Reckless Rash*; I was only sorry that Lady Vanessa Sherwin-Williams' bodice-busting adventures with the Duke of Earl, Beau Weevil, Trapper Jacques and the rest didn't go on for hundreds more pages!"

—Carol McD. Wallace
Co-author of *The Preppie Handbook*

Love's
Reckless
Rash

Future Charlatan Romances
by Rosemary Cartwheel

SWEET AND SOUR LOVE
HOT AND SPICY LOVE
DAMP, MOIST LOVE
SWEET, SWEATY LOVE
SWEET, SAVAGE MENOPAUSE
BALD, BREATHLESS LOVE
HOT LOVE, BIG LOVE
BY GEORGE, IT'S LOVE
MARXIST LOVE, HEGELIAN LOVE

Love's Reckless Rash

by ROSEMARY CARTWHEEL

A Charlatan Romance

St. Martin's Press / New York

Design by Laura Hammond Hough

Library of Congress Cataloging in Publication Data

Cartwheel, Rosemary
   Love's reckless rash.

   (A Charlatan romance)
   I. Title.
PS3553.A7845L6   1984   813'.54   83-24646
ISBN 0-312-49971-X

First Edition

10 9 8 7 6 5 4 3 2 1

"I love you," she said, caressing his elbow as if it were the very center of his Being. A strong sea wind blew her long auburn hair into his face, and momentarily blinded, he pulled her to him and lifted her chin slightly so that her lips were poised to meet his. As they kissed, she was transported through Time Eternal to another plain of Being.

"I love you more than I have ever loved anything or anyone in my life," he said as the breeze made her long ebony hair slap him mercilessly about the head. Gently spitting her hair out of his mouth, he kissed her again and again. Soon she became conscious of something hard and firm pressing against her tender loins.

"Your sword," she whispered in his ear. "Your sword is making a dent in my Person."

But it was not his sword, as she would find out later. It was his pistol. . . .

Vanessa: Her restless Beauty was flawed only by a small, heart-shaped rash. Was it a royal mark of distinction or a curse, fating her to an exile far, far from her One True Love? Or what?

The Young Duke: Handsome, dashing, debonair, he was a wealthy heir and an excellent dancer—and he vowed to love Vanessa for Time Eternal or the rest of his life, whichever came first.

The Riverboat Gambler: Rich, wealthy, and well-off, he was there when Vanessa needed him—but he didn't have his steamboat paddle completely in the water.

The Fur Trapper: He was a ruthless cad—and after months in the wilderness, *not* a shining example of personal hygiene—but his passion drove him wild.

The Lonely Monk: His vow of silence kept him from revealing a terrible secret to Vanessa. His vows of poverty and chastity weren't much fun, either. Would he break his silence or perish with the secret?

BOOK I

Fate Takes a Savage Turn

♡   ♡   ♡

Two souls with but a single thought,
Two hearts that beat as one,
Two pairs of feet e'er side by side
Else they wouldst trip o'er one ano'er.
                                        —*Anonymous*

Chapter 1

♡   ♡   ♡

$\mathcal{L}$ady Vanessa Sherwin-Williams awoke that morning feeling both reckless and passionate. Although she had awakened feeling one way or the other every day since puberty, the fact that she had awakened feeling *both* meant that today was going to be a special day.

She did not awaken suddenly, for she had been immersed in a dream so rapturous, so tempestuous, so passionate, so timeless, so filled with the manifold ecstasies of love that she surely would have swooned had she not already been asleep. Now blinking her long-lashed Delft-blue eyes once or twice to remember where she was, a saucy smile played across her full, lush, supple, ruby-red, heart-shaped lips as she recalled the rhapsody to which her nocturnal trance had transported her. She had dreamt, as she did every night, that a tall, mysterious stranger had swept her up onto his dashing white steed, his arm firm and strong as it encircled her slight, perfect waist, and had carried her across the foggy moors to a lush, Eden-like glade, where they had alighted and at once declared their everlasting love for each other while birds twittered in the trees and the dashing white steed relieved itself in the moss. He had pulled her to him impetuously, and though she had tried to restrain him, he was too irresistible to withstand and so she had given in to his fiery caresses. He had crushed her pliant body to his and . . . and . . .

But then she had been awakened by a shaft of sunlight rudely penetrating the curtains of her bedroom window, and the rapturous trance had dissolved, transporting her back to reality.

As she arose, placing one foot upon the delicate carpet of Persian wool, then another foot, then another, a warm sense of anticipation permeated her perfect body and a smile as beautiful as life itself played upon her always-moist lips. This was, she remembered suddenly, the day of the Duchess of Winston's Masquerade Ball, the most important event of the Devonshire social season. Everyone would be there, virtually the entire peerage of the realm: the Lord of Marlborough, the Duke of Kent, the Earl of Tareyton, the Marquis of Chesterfield, both the Dukes of Benson and of Hedges. And, yes, Vanessa would be there, too!

It was to be her first ball. True, she would not be wearing as beautiful a gown as her three sisters. And, true, she would not get to see what her escort looked like until this evening, when he would come by in his carriage to pick her up. But she was going at last! After all the years of drudgery, of sitting at home in the castle playing endless games of solitaire, or that fashionable new game from France, "Toss the Toast," while her half sisters went to all the balls and galas, she, the eldest daughter of Lord Sherwin-Williams, was finally going to have a night of her own! Her father, so often intimidated by her sisters, had given his assent secretly, provided she went with young Lord Gastleigh, whom she had never met. And if her gown did not meet the fashion standard of her sisters, she was certain her Beauty would make up for it.

For Beauty was something she possessed in a way that few had ever possessed it before. She was the very definition of the word. Green eyes the color and texture of the most precious sapphires blazed like yellow beacons from aquamarine sockets. A flawlessly patrician nose separated those eyes from an equally flawless set of full, lush, supple, ruby-red, heart-shaped lips that, when parted, allowed her to speak or consume food. Pitch-black hair the color of willow bark cascaded from her slender forehead, and the russet tresses floated down to her shoulders, which were like alabaster in the morning sun, though more like the finest marble by moonlight. She was Beauty personified, an uncanny combination of Venus and Aphrodite.

How beautiful was her Beauty? It was a Beauty so heart-stopping that the spindly old Duc de Beaujolais, on a visit from Versailles, spotted her on the streets of Devonshire one afternoon and promptly toppled headfirst onto the cobblestones, later to be pronounced dead of heart stoppage.

But Beauty, as she knew only too well, could also be a curse. Unfortunately, Lady Vanessa's three half sisters had not been graced with a beauty as remarkable as hers, and though Vanessa felt only kindness toward them, their envy and jealousy of her occasionally showed. When the old Lord wasn't looking, which was much of the time, due to his various distractions, her sisters had a tendency to treat Vanessa like a common scullery maid, ordering her to scrub floors and dressing her in rags inappropriate to her family's wealth and station, and that were completely out of fashion anyway.

Was it her fault that her natural Beauty had lured her sisters' suitors away, one after the other? Was she to blame that Lady Agnes had always seemed somewhat plump about the ankles? Or that Lady Gertrude had, at birth, been more or less deprived of a neck? Or that Divine Providence had made her third sister, Lady Ralph, both taller and wider than most of the castle doorways?

She could only hope that her father, never considered the swiftest peer in the county, would be able to rouse himself to get the sisters suitable husbands. Only then would she have her freedom! Only then would she find True Love!

But in the meantime, she knew that she had to cater to the fanciful whims of her three stepsisters, and with that in mind, she threw on her shabby gingham dress and slipped into a pair of old pighide slippers. There was much to do—for one thing, she had to prepare for the arrival of a quaint little tailor she had summoned in secrecy. It was he who would provide her with a gown for this evening. She also had to clean out the chamber pots and then cook breakfast for her sisters.

Tripping quietly downstairs so as not to awaken anybody, then picking herself up, Vanessa was overjoyed to see that her father was in what was for him a fairly alert state. He was sitting upright in his elegant, mahogany-lined study, tapping himself briskly on the forehead with the venerable family scepter, a hobby that had absorbed much of his time since Lady Vanessa's mother, his beloved wife, had expired eighteen years earlier. Catching sight of his radiantly beautiful daughter, the old Lord averted his eyes, for he had a weak heart.

"Dear Vanessa, you must be awake already!" he exclaimed, staring at a priceless tapestry hanging on the wall, a mere trifle he had picked up in Bayeux.

"Oh, Papa!" Lady Vanessa replied happily. "I am indeed awake, as my presence before you testifies. I daresay I could not sleep another wink, for today I am in higher spirits than ever before!"

"And why, pray tell, is that?" the kindly old Duke asked.

"Surely you haven't forgotten, Father," she said. "Tonight

is the Rose and Thorn Masquerade—the eighth ball given by the Duchess of Winston this season!"

"Ah, yes," the old Lord said. "The Duchess certainly has a lot of balls."

"I have heard that said about her, Papa," said Vanessa. "But this will be my very first ball and I can hardly contain my excitement!"

"Yes, but you must promise me again not to breathe a word of it to your sisters," the old Lord whispered. "If they were to find out I had given you my permission to attend this affair, they would make my life miserable."

"I promise, Father," said Vanessa in a voice that was filled to the brim with sincerity. "I have arranged for the tailor to meet me by the Crooked Tree while my sisters are dressing. By the time Lord Gastleigh's carriage arrives, they will have already left."

"Splendid," the old gentleman said. "Just make sure that you do not remove your mask at the ball. I have told Lord Gastleigh that he should also remain masked, to avoid any possibility of heinous wrath."

"Yes, Papa," said Vanessa pleasantly, "though I regret that I will not be able to see all of Lord Gastleigh's fine, handsome features behind his mask."

Her kind father cleared his throat nervously.

"I imagine he is extremely handsome and dashing," Vanessa said dreamily, falling into a slight rapture.

"One might say he is handsome and dashing," said the Lord slowly, "but in sooth I cannot say I have actually heard him described so."

"And tall," Lady Vanessa continued. "I'll wager he is tall. And strong, very strong." The thin, sensuous cloth of her blouse began sticking to her skin. She felt her rapture increase somewhat, and a quiver ran through her perfect body. "I'll also wager that his shoulders are broad and . . ."

7

"I would counsel you against rushing into such a wager, my dear," averred the old Lord helpfully.

"Then is he slender, Father?" Vanessa asked, her breath coming short and heavy.

The old gentleman coughed several times. "Everything is relative, my dear. Is the swine slender when compared with an elephant?"

"Yes," Lady Vanessa replied brightly, sensing this was the beginning of one of her father's clever riddles.

"But is the elephant slender when compared to a gnat?"

"No."

"Then there is your answer," said the kindly Lord.

"How very, very clever you are, Papa!" Lady Vanessa gushed. "But . . ."

"Enough questions, my dearest," the old gentleman said with that firmness he could summon up from time to time. "Soon your sisters will be lumbering downstairs. You should hie yourself hence." With that, the old peer picked up his beloved family scepter and resumed his habitual pastime.

Her blush still fading, Lady Vanessa happily gathered up her skirts and bounded girlishly from the study, the rhythmic *thwack, thwack* of the scepter following her out the door.

♡　　　　♡　　　　♡

Lady Vanessa thought the afternoon would never end. Her three sisters kept her busy with all manner of menial tasks so they could rest for the Grand Ball. But she went about her chores with a pleasant humor, and a smile of anticipation never left her face, not even while she massaged the unusually large bunions on Lady Gertrude's feet.

Still, her sisters could not resist cruelly taunting her. " 'Tis a shame you shan't go to the ball," Lady Agnes brayed. "Everyone above a Viscount will be there."

"I hear that even the Prince may attend," Lady Gertrude mumbled, dribbling cake crumbs down her ample bodice.

"Even more exciting than that," rasped Lady Ralph, "rumor has it that the Duke . . . of *Earl* will be in attendance!" The sisters all gasped. As everyone in Devonshire knew, the Duke of Earl was the most charming, the most sought-after—and the most elusive—man in the county. Even dutiful Vanessa, who did not indulge in idle chatter, had heard of the notorious Duke of Earl. Women repeatedly fell at his feet, scuffing his shoes, and it was even whispered that several had committed suicide— of an overdose of epsom salts—after being spurned by the young Duke. So many men had challenged him over affairs of honor that he had been compelled to keep a waiting list. If that weren't enough, he was also an accomplished horseman, a first-rate swordsman, and the luckiest gambler in the realm.

He must be awfully conceited, Vanessa thought as her stepsisters indulged in gossip about the young Duke. She pictured him as a bloated, somewhat pompous man with long whiskers who would probably speak dully and at great length on subjects that bored her—cards and horses and life. Yet, in her heart of hearts, she was curious about the undoubtedly arrogant Duke and wondered if she would ever meet him.

Vanessa scrubbed out the privies with good cheer. It was a task her sisters gave her when the servants were off, as they were today, to attend the public hanging later that afternoon of a notorious bread-roll thief. Even her own lady's maid, the French-born Brigitte, had decided to attend, for advance word among the servant class had it that the thief might be drawn and quartered as well. As she toiled, she listened virtuously to her sisters' slanderous gossip.

"D'you suppose the Duke of Earl is anything like his late father?" Lady Agnes grunted.

"Oh, my, those rumors! He was quite a ladies' man, wasn't he?" asked Lady Gertrude crudely. "Still, nothing as bad as his son, the young Duke of Earl. Rumor has it"—her voice dropped to a coarse whisper—"that he has violated the purity of several county virgins."

A hush fell over the three sisters as each of them pondered the fortunate local ex-virgins.

"I wonder how he'll be hung?" said Lady Ralph dreamily.

"What?" her sisters chorused.

"The bread-roll thief," said Lady Ralph. "From a gibbet? From a gallows? Drawn and quartered? I do hope they aren't coddling them this month."

"Oh," said Lady Agnes, much relieved.

"Anyway," Lady Ralph opined, "that young Duke is certainly a bounder!"

"A blackguard!"

"A rake!"

"A hoe!"

The three sisters looked at Vanessa, who had uttered this last declamation. "What, pray tell, is a *hoe?*" Lady Ralph asked witheringly.

Vanessa blushed. "A hoe," she said weakly. "You know, like a rake, only without teeth."

At that, the sisters dissolved into loud, sputtering, snorting giggles and it took all of Vanessa's Christian charity *not* to think of the sounds made by the hogs when her sisters forced her to slop them. She tried to banish the thought from her mind. I'll think about Love and Beauty and Passion instead, Vanessa said to herself, and soon the snorting laughter of the sisters faded as Vanessa was once again transported into a semitempestuous rapture.

♡   ♡   ♡

Late that afternoon, as her sisters lolled abed to rest before the ball, Vanessa hied herself to the Crooked Tree at one end of her father's magnificent estate. She had told the funny little tailor she would meet him here at four, and it was almost that o'clock now. She looked about with sincere concern. Where was he? She had chanced to meet him when she had mistakenly taken a carriage ride through the unkempt Lower East Side of Devonshire. Since her fine eye for craftsmanship, as for Beauty, was undeterred by mere squalor, she immediately noticed the quality and variety of the cloths he exhibited outside his wretched hut. A bargain for a newly sewn gown was quickly struck, and he had promised to deliver the finished dress this afternoon. Still, what odd people these Jewish tradesmen were! She had of course recognized him as being of the Hebrew faith because of his looks and because he could add sums without moving his lips. But where *was* the fellow?

Her doubts were relieved anon when, at the stroke of four, she spotted the tailor's horse trotting around a bend in the road. She should have trusted her own convictions! The little fellow drew near, dismounted, shook the dust from a strange beanie he sported on his pate by slapping the little thing once or twice on his knee, and greeted Lady Vanessa.

"*Nu?*" he inquired.

Before she could reply (had she even known how to answer such an odd greeting), he had produced a swath of brilliant crimson from his carrying case and displayed it before her.

"It's . . . it's beautiful!" she exlaimed. It was her gown, in gorgeous red brocade, with sequins and lace and—she was quick to notice—it was daringly low-cut. She knew at once that she would go to the ball that evening as the mysterious Lady in Red. She clasped her heart in gratitude. "It's a work of . . . Art!" she exclaimed delightedly.

"Not quite," the tailor said. "It's a work of Murray, to be precise."

"I'm so happy," Vanessa cried, "so very, very happy!"

"Mazel Tov," the tailor said, "but to tell you the truth, Lady, I almost had a heart stoppage coming to this *meshuggeneh* place. I'm riding along, minding my own business, when this glassy-eyed bloke jumps out of the moors, right in front of my horse. What a nerve! Does he stop? Does he say, 'Pardon me'? No! He just wanders around like a crazy man, moaning 'Cathy . . . Cathy' over and over again."

"Oh, you mustn't worry about *him,*" Lady Vanessa said, laughing gaily. "That's just the county character, Heathcliff. He's been doing that for years."

"Heathcliff, Shmeathcliff, he ought to be locked up, that bloke. He's a definite traffic hazard."

But Lady Vanessa did not hear him. Gazing at her gown, thinking of the evening to come, imagining the fine features of Lord Gastleigh and their approaching encounter, she had once again been transported to about three-quarters rapture. Concerned, the tailor waved his hand in front of her glassy eyes, but Vanessa, entranced, only stared dreamily into the distance.

"Everybody's *meshuggeneh* around here," the tailor uttered to himself and, without bidding his beautiful patroness adieu, mounted his horse and rode off. As for Vanessa, she rode confidently but rapturously homeward—and to the destiny that awaited her.

Chapter

2

♡ ♡ ♡

_N_ight fell, as it had for centuries, and Lady Vanessa took advantage of a few free moments to take a sensuous, languorous bath. The Grand Ball was only a couple of hours away and her sisters were busy being corsetted, winched, and crowbarred into their ball gowns. Her own crimson creation was tucked discreetly in her closet, so for now she let the soap and water flow in gentle rivulets along the contours of her soft, velvety, flesh-colored skin. Her body was, of course, flawless, except for a strange birthmark on the back of her left thigh. Defects of any sort disturbed her and she had tried many times to make this attractive stigma disappear. It was not a mole, nor a freckle, nor—perish the very idea!—a zit. It was a red spot, pink in hue, the size of a Spanish gold piece. Appropriately, considering Vanessa's sweet nature, it was in the shape of a heart. As a child she had thought it was merely a rash, and perhaps that is just what it was; but none of the rash remedies prescribed by her physician had succeeded in removing it. The best Vanessa was able to do was to cover it up with her own secret makeup—a clever concoction of attar of roses and horse glue.

Delicately, she stepped out of her tub and walked naked into her bedchamber, lit only by a clear, white shaft of moonlight that penetrated the window curtains. By the light of the silvery moon, she gazed out her window and saw three carriages being valet-parked in front of the Sherwin-Williams Castle. Her sisters' escorts had arrived on time! She must hurry, for soon *her* prince, the dashing Lord Gastleigh, would be here to sweep her away to the ball—and, perhaps, to Love Eternal!

Applying first a delicate film of soft white powder to her perfectly proportioned anatomy, she then daubed herself with perfume and carefully removed her evening gown from its hanger. As she did thus, she could hear her sisters' voices below, followed by the snorting and neighing of the horses, then the snorting and neighing of her sisters, then the loud clattering departure of the carriages.

When she was certain they were gone, she summoned her lady's maid, Brigitte.

"Brigitte, come hither," she called melodiously. The French domestic had been recently hired by her kindly old father when it became obvious that Vanessa needed *some* help to compensate for the legions of downstairs staff who waited on her sisters. Brigitte was back from the hanging, and in fine spirits.

"Oy'm 'ere, moydmezelle," said Brigitte in that odd little accent that domestics from the French provinces apparently had. She came shambling in from the antechamber, a stout girl with red cheeks and redder knuckles.

"Please help me into this gown, Brigitte," said Vanessa sweetly, "and as always, I rely on your discretion."

"Eh?" Brigitte screwed up her massive forehead in a vivid display of confusion. Vanessa understood with a sympathetic smile that foreigners could not be expected to understand the subtleties of the English tongue. After all, her own French tutor had decided when she was younger that, as a student of the French tongue, Vanessa's abilities were perhaps better directed toward home economics or embroidery. So the sympathy between mistress and maid, Vanessa often felt, went deeper than the ordinary class relationship, even if comprehension was often murky. Still, the important thing was that Brigitte was French, as all good English ladies' maids were required to be.

"Discretion," said Vanessa. "You keep . . . secret, yes?"

A dim light of perception flickered in the girl's eyes. "Aww, sure, an' the mistress mus' mean her three bloody sisters! Naah, Oy'd never breathe a word, Mistress Vanessa!" Then, after a pause, the outspoken French domestic added, *"Seal Voos plate!"* This was one of the things Vanessa found most interesting about her maid: She didn't at all sound as if she were speaking the kind of Parisian French she remembered from her tutor. Doubtless Brigitte was from an exotic part of France, such as Normandy or Sicily.

With the help of Brigitte, Vanessa slipped into her gown and gazed into a long mirror by her bed to study her appearance. What she saw not only resembled her closely, but pleased her immensely. It was a beautiful gown, as beautiful as life itself, and it brought out the color of those flashing emerald eyes, sparkling like sapphires in the golden moonlight. It would be a shame to diminish the impact of such topaz-colored eyes with a mask, but it had to be thus. Perhaps she would playfully give Lord Gastleigh a peek behind her disguise as they drove back later that night. Perhaps he would give her a peek, too, behind his virile mask. Perhaps he would reach across the carriage seat and pull her toward him. Perhaps he would plant a kiss on her cheek. Perhaps it would grow. Perhaps—

The loud clatter of a carriage pulling up below her window interrupted her momentary reverie, making this the sixth incomplete reverie she had experienced that day.

" 'Ey, it mus' be your bloke, missy!" said Brigitte, adding

quickly, *"Sacre blarney!"* She laced the final eyeholes of her mistress's gown as Vanessa chuckled at her maid's quaint French expressions. But as she realized that Brigitte was right, that it probably was Lord Gastleigh, her amusement changed to something else. . . . An excitement she had never known before penetrated every pore of her young, nearly perfect body. She scurried over to the window and beheld, double-parked before the castle door, a splendid white carriage. As the carriage door began to open, a quiver went through her, like a blaze flickering in a fire. But she mustn't stand there and keep the young Lord waiting! Without further ado, she took her mask, placed it gently over her bewitching eyes, and hied herself from her chamber.

"Shank o' the evenin' to ya, missy!" shouted Brigitte. "Or, as we Frenchies say, *Frères Jacques!*"

With breathless anticipation, Vanessa tiptoed gracefully down the corridor. At the top of the long, winding staircase she paused. A dizzying swoon threatened to envelop her, and although swoons were pretty much a matter of routine to Vanessa, she knew from past experience that swooning at high altitudes could be perilous to a person's Person. Once, months before, she had stood atop a moorish crest above the local cesspond, reading aloud from a new romantic novel by the Dutch writer, Dostoevski. Rapture had overcome her at this benighted high spot, and she had tumbled gracefully into the brack water below, soiling her entire Person. This unlucky experience had taught her well to endure rapture at altitudes far closer to sea level.

Holding the banister to reestablish both the poise and the

equilibrium that were her birthright, Vanessa waited until the dizzying rapture subsided, then proceeded with natural grace down the stairs. It was her plan to catch a secret glimpse of Lord Gastleigh before being formally introduced to him. In this way, she would be able to surmise the kind of man he was and comport herself accordingly. Not for nothing had she spent all those moonlit evenings reading of the wiles of Women in Love in those delicious romantic novels. If Lord Gastleigh were dashing, she knew she should be coy; if he were bold, she would be demure; if he were forward, she would be backward; if he were bashful, she would be bashless. . . .

At the foot of the stairs she gracefully ceased descending. She peered through the crack in the door that led into the Great Parlour. Yes, he was there, speaking in quiet tones with her beloved father. But was he dashing and handsome? Alas, it was extraordinarily difficult to tell as Lord Gastleigh was down on all fours, disguised as a large bloodhound. The costume, brown with dark spots, was cleverly conceived, but Vanessa could not stifle a momentary flash of disappointment. If Lord Gastleigh was going to stick to his canine demeanor, it would be difficult to be swept away by ardor, much less get a good bead on the nobleman's charm, personality, or height.

Thankfully, Lord Gastleigh stood up straight and crossed his paws to observe her father perform a magickal trick. This was something the old Duke loved to do—entertain guests with feats of magick and alchemy—and it allowed Vanessa to see that Lord Gastleigh was of average height and of above-average rotundity. Her father, fetchingly disguised as a rooster, asked the young Lord to "loan" him a one thousand-pound note. Lord Gastleigh, his hound's ears flapping with amusement, reached into a specially sewn pocket and brought out his purse. Extracting a fresh bank note, he handed it to the Duke, who crumpled the note and flung it into the fireplace, where it magickally burst into flame. Lord Gastleigh howled in pleasure and clapped his paws, and even Vanessa could hardly resist a chuckle at this delightful trick.

At last, she left her hiding place and swept into the Grand Parlour. She was a vision in red and crimson, and not at all unaware of the impression she was about to make. . . .

"Ta-da!" She announced to the room at large.

"Do you have any more tricks like that, Your Grace?" asked Lord Gastleigh, scratching his hind leg.

Disappointment coursed through Vanessa like embers being doused. Was this the dashing prince her fertile mind had envisioned? An overfed bloodhound who took no notice of her dramatic entrance? Moreover, she could see through the holes in the dog's-head mask that Lord Gastleigh's eyes were askew. There was no getting around it: Though the costume tended to conceal it, Lord Gastleigh was definitely walleyed. This was not a promising start to the most rapturous adventure in Vanessa's life!

Yet, as befitted a lady of her station, Vanessa vowed to hide her disappointment and to be as gracious and courteous as she could. Even if it meant leaning down to talk to him, or tugging at the oversize leash she was apparently meant to hold throughout the evening, she would strive to bring out the finer qualities she was sure Lord Gastleigh possessed.

After clearing her lovely throat loudly a few times, Vanessa finally made herself noticed.

"Ah, my dear daughter," said her father, as always averting his eyes from her heart-stopping Beauty. "Allow me to present our family friend, Lord Gastleigh."

"What a clever costume, Lord Gastleigh," exclaimed Vanessa, extending her delicate hand. The portly bloodhound bowed to kiss it, slobbering as he did so.

"Thank you most kindly, dear lady," came a whiny, nasal

voice from inside the dog's snout. "May I say that you are the very picture of Beauty?"

"You may."

"You are the very picture of Beauty."

"Thank you, kind sir," Vanessa said, wiping her hand on her gown.

"And what about your father, dear?" asked the kindly old Duke, strutting about proudly in his rooster costume. "What do you think of *my* disguise?"

"Never have I seen a more noble Cock," Vanessa cried happily. "You will surely be the best Cock of the Ball!"

"Then we had better hie there hence," the kindly old Duke said, and the three ballgoers adjusted their masks and dispatched themselves to Lord Gastleigh's waiting coach.

♡ ♡ ♡

As the carriage clattered down the long, winding dirt road to the Duchess's castle, the kindly old Duke explained how Vanessa should keep her identity concealed at the ball. It was, of course, necessary that Lady Agnes, Lady Gertrude, and Lady Ralph be kept unaware of Vanessa's presence. Otherwise, there would be the devil to pay.

"You will be announced as . . . as . . . as the Baroness of Pigalle," exclaimed the old gentleman, groping for the only French place-name he could recall from his youth. French was the language of elegance and distinction in this era of English history, and the kindly old Duke correctly sensed that Vanessa would be above suspicion if she adopted such a distinguished-sounding title. "As the Baroness of Pigalle, you must keep your mask on at all times and say nothing that might betray your identity."

Vanessa wished she had her lady's maid, Brigitte, with her to coach her in French manners, but dutifully promised to obey her father's commands. Above all, she did not wish him to suffer the heinous wrath of her sisters should they discover the truth. The old gentleman's heart, she well knew, could not stand much heinous wrath. In fact, after his last seizure, the physician had specifically instructed Vanessa to make sure she kept heinous wrath to a minimum. Thus, Vanessa swore to her father she would preserve the secret, and the kindly old Duke was able to doze off, happily plumping his feathers beneath him.

This meant Vanessa was left with the burden of entertaining Lord Gastleigh for the duration of the journey, but since she did not recall the etiquette of conversing with a canine nobleman in a rolling carriage, she was at a loss for words. Fortunately Lord Gastleigh was not.

"Arf," he said.

Vanessa tittered politely, not knowing what to make of his remark. Lord Gastleigh apparently took the art of masquerade quite seriously.

"Indeed," she replied noncommittally.

"Would you care for a nip?" he asked, reaching into his pocket for a flask. Vanessa breathed a sigh of relief. At least he did not intend to stay in character all evening!

"Why, yes, thank you," she said, pleased. A ladylike sip of spirits was no impropriety.

At that, Lord Gastleigh immediately leaned over and nipped at her lily-white shoulder.

"Woof!" Lord Gastleigh barked with canine delight.

Lady Vanessa sighed. This did not bode well for the evening to come. As was her wont in such situations, she allowed herself to drift into a reverie. Lulled by the carriage's motion, she dreamt that the coach had stopped and that Lord

Gastleigh had jumped out to bay at the moon. Dogless, she proceeded on to the ball and made her grand entrance. There, amid the swirl of color and music, she dreamt that she captivated the attentions of a handsome and strong cavalier, disguised in a costume far more noble and dignified than a bloodhound—that of a golden retriever, or a French poodle, perhaps. Then, before she knew it, they were dancing, whirling about, her feet lighter than air, their hearts beating as one, their eyes locked together so tightly that no key could unlock them.

In this ethereal mist, the Mysterious Cavalier had led her toward a quiet nook, where they looked deeply into each other's eyes and both saw the same thing—eyes. His embrace was like a warm caress and his caress very much like a warm embrace. He took her chin in his firm yet resolute hand. Her lips parted in anticipation of the Kiss he was about to bestow. He moved closer, his own mouth opening as . . .

"Dash it all!" came a whiny voice. "I think I have fleas!"

Rudely, Vanessa was transported back to reality by the sight of the affronted Lord Gastleigh scratching madly at his midsection with a large, padded foot. She blinked as the reverie faded and nudged the rooster, her kindly old father, awake. It was time: Outside the carriage, the Duchess's castle—and destiny itself—loomed before them.

Chapter 3

♡ ♡ ♡

*N*ever in her life had Vanessa seen anything quite as exquisite as the Duchess's ballroom. Never had she seen so many women so splendidly groomed. Never had she seen so much jewelry, sparkling and clanking. Never had she seen so many noblemen cleverly disguised as domestic animals, assorted fowl, and common vegetables. There, standing by a fine Doric column, was a wealthy Viscount who had once visited her father, decked out tonight most interestingly as a beet. The air was alive with a gaiety so palpable that Vanessa could almost smell it. Then she realized the odor came from the uplifted arms and tufts presented by their hostess the Duchess, who was rushing toward them.

"Your Grace!" rumbled the Duchess. "How perfectly splendid to see you!" She threw her beefy arms around the kindly old Duke, scattering feathers upon the exquisite marble floor. Stepping back, the stout Duchess peered through her eyeglass at Vanessa.

"I know three of your daughters have already arrived," she said, "but who could this be?"

"Ah . . . this is the Baroness of Pigalle," he said, madly winking his rooster eye at Vanessa. "She is from . . . France."

At that, the Duchess descended massively into a deep curtsy.

"Soyez la bienvenue, Madame la Baronesse," said the Duchess. *"Nous sommes enchantés de vous recevoir."*

Vanessa felt panic well up in her perfect yet modest breast. If only Brigitte were here! What would she say in a situation like this? What did she remember from her tutor? Oh oh . . . oh . . . it was coming back to her!

"Alouette, gentille alouette," she said brightly. *"Alouette, je te plumerai."*

The Duchess looked at Vanessa peculiarly through her lorgnette, scratched some stubble on her chin, and moved away, mumbling amenities. Vanessa was safe!

Confidently, Vanessa surveyed the ballroom. What her sisters had said about this particular gala was true: The aristocracy had turned out! Why, wasn't that the Count of Basie over there by the pianoforte? And wasn't that the Duke of Ellington, looking a bit melancholy, his mood somewhat indigo? And there was the Earl of Worcestershire, sauced as usual. Oh, there were Earls, and Dukes and Counts and Princes everywhere tonight! The music was lively and international—at this moment a French gavotte known as "Le Lavabo des Tuileries" was being played—and both the ladies and the gentlemen danced together. Since this was not always the case, it was clear this ball was destined to be a success.

Before she knew it, the tempo of the music had changed—to the beat of a newer Prussian minuet called "Der Schmutz der Führer"—and Lord Gastleigh had swept her up in his large paws and was twirling her around the floor. Soon they were spinning in the center of the floor, pausing every so often, as was the Prussian custom, to kick each other sharply on the shins to the roll of the drums. Though caught up entirely in the dizzying swirl of the minuet, Vanessa glanced around the room. She felt a slight, guilty pleasure at seeing her three sisters standing together, like potted plants, at the edge of the dance floor. How envious they would be if they knew it was she, laughing gaily as she kicked her partner, the center of attention, a radiant vision of crimson loveliness!

After several dances, Lord Gastleigh was perspiring through his fur, and besides that he was beginning to lift one hind leg up in the air in a disconcerting fashion, so Vanessa suggested he hie himself to the men's privy to "wash up." He agreed, but bade Vanessa remain where she was standing and promised to return forthwith.

Alone, Vanessa watched her escort push a couple of footmen aside and stride through the exquisite paneled doors. Catching her breath, she leaned against a marble column and surveyed the gorgeous ballroom, awash with bright hues and general merriment. But suddenly, as if guided by a celestial spirit, her golden-brown eyes lit upon the figure of a man across the room. For some reason, she could not remove her eyes from his Person, no matter how hard she tried. Whenever she attempted to avert them in a ladylike fashion, some force greater than any she had ever known caused them to return to his direction. It was as if her eyes were small iron balls and his Person a magnet, drawing her eyes forth from her skull and causing them to roll across the dance floor to his Person.

Dressed as a jaunty but fashionable buccaneer, complete with spyglass and cutlass, the Mysterious Stranger was at once the most handsome man she had ever gazed upon, and also the best-looking. His demeanor was that of a gentle rogue well accustomed to the attentions of ladies of all ages, as well as of animals and certain larger plants. The careless pose of his hips and the slight curl of his lip told her that much. Instinctively, however, she knew he was also kind, forbearing, a good dancer, excellent with children, and could hum in perfect pitch, but at the same time was noble and manly, well-mannered and tall, very tall.

Suddenly, as if guided by a similar celestial spirit, the Mysterious Stranger's eyes lifted from the throng of adoring women that surrounded him and glanced directly at Vanessa. Shyly she attempted to avert her sapphire eyes, but it was to no avail. Their eyes were suddenly drawn to each other and held, as if by some heavenly glue with a special bonding agent. Nothing mortal could separate their eyes, that was for sure. Vanessa began to feel the familiar stirrings of a rapture come upon her.

As they continued to stare at each other, suddenly he broke off . . . curled his lip and . . . *laughed!* It was the last thing Vanessa expected. She began to blush deeply scarlet, blending in tastefully with her gown, her rapture turning to anger, resentment, and outright miffedness. What right did the bounder have to laugh at their private moment, to mock the feelings that threatened to engulf her?

She had no idea who the masked buccaneer was, but whatever his provenance, she would make sure he did not get another chance to have the upper hand—or eye, in this case. Angrily, Vanessa flounced away from the column and strode toward the priceless leaded windows that led to the courtyard outside. Swishing past the passive footmen, she practically ran into the warm, moonlit air, a tear glistening in her eyes. It was one thing to be taken advantage of by her sisters, she thought, but quite another to be humiliated by an arrogant buccaneer at a gala ball!

Her angry reverie was interrupted by a deep voice.

"I wasn't laughing *at* you," said a deeply sensitive yet unmistakably virile voice. "I was laughing *with* you." There was a pause. Vanessa dared not turn around. The voice said one more thing: "And I think . . . I'm in love with you."

Vanessa did not move a muscle in her perfect body. She did not breathe. As the moment stretched out interminably, into a bliss she had never dared think possible, the lack of breath became a problem, and so she resumed inhaling.

Could it be? Could this be real? Had this deep, virile voice really spoken those lovely words, the very words she had so often dreamt of hearing? Or was she merely confusing the real with the imaginary? Was it possible that, unwittingly, she had been transported into a reverie? *Again?*

Steeling herself, because copper had gotten expensive, Vanessa was almost afraid to find out the truth for fear that the voice, and its speaker, would turn out to be nothing more than a glorious apparition, taunting her with words of ardor. Yet, as she stood there transfixed, still not daring to face him, she could feel his eyes insolently surveying her raven hair and she found herself hoping, with all of her Being, that she did not have what Brigitte referred to as *les petites dandruffes.*

Trembling, she closed her eyes tightly and spun around on her heels to face her mysterious admirer. Then she opened her eyes and found that she had perhaps spun a trifle too far: She was now facing the open mouth of a yawning footman. Turning more slowly, her gaze finally fell upon the dashing buccaneer. He was leaning rakishly against a bashful but stocky wallflower, gazing at Vanessa with piercing grey eyes. Not for him a gaudy and obvious pirate's costume: He wore instead a subtly ruffled shirt open to his chest, and above the pocket was a tiny emblem—an alligator with an eyepatch. His tall frame loomed above her, casting a long shadow over her lithe, slender, perfect body.

The strains of an achingly beautiful Italian air, "Fungili Fan Tutti," wafted out the ballroom doors. Without a word, he held up his arm for Vanessa to take. Her heart pounding like a blacksmith's hammer, she moved gracefully beside him as they went back into the ballroom and began to dance. As he crushed her pliant body to his, she felt helpless to combat the raging fires he had started. But she knew that it was she herself who was fanning the blaze of passion! This was a rapture Vanessa had never before experienced, flaming in its intensity, smoky in its fragrance. She knew instinctively that she was either close to falling in love or she was developing a tendency toward pyromania.

As the familiar celestial spirit began to guide them, they danced around the ballroom floor, oblivious to the people around them, to the lights and colors and sounds, to life itself. She felt herself floating above the room, caressed by warm air, dodging the chandeliers, soaring through fragrant clouds. She knew only that the rapture and ecstasy of it was out of time and might have lasted a few seconds or many centuries. (Not to take anything away from the moment, but the truth was that Vanessa had *always* been poor at estimating time. Once, after a lesson, her tutor had asked her to estimate how long ago she thought dinosaurs had roamed the earth, and Vanessa had ventured, "Thirty-five years?")

Presently, she was one with the handsome stranger, their bodies moving as if pinned together, round and round, until she felt she would surely swoon. His strong arms, bristling with skin, gripped her feminine body about the waist and she was entirely in his control. All else had faded into an ethereal mist, and they were dancing alone, peering at each other through the sublime fog.

And yet, and yet . . . they still said nothing to each other. They spoke only with their eyes, in a language understood only by lovers and optometrists.

His eyes spoke first: "You are the most beautiful creature ever born on the face of the earth."

"You are too kind," her eyes retorted.

His eyes continued: "You are more beautiful than the first vernal bloom of Spring upon the lake, more delicious than the Autumn harvest's first berry, more pleasingly scented than the wild flowers of Summer that bespeckle the heathrow." His eyelashes paused as they took stock of the seasons: He had missed one. "Hmmm," said his eyes. "Oh, yes . . . and more beautiful than a melted snowlake upon a Winter loon." Gaining confidence, his eyes rushed on: "I love you more than words can say, more than the billions and billions of stars in the heavens, more than the sparkling grains of sand on the shore."

It was obvious that his eyes were more talkative than hers and she drank in their utterances as if they were silver chalices of the purest red wine. Yet even though his eye-talk was more eloquent than any she had ever seen, she wished his eyes would give her a break, and that he would take her away from all this so they could begin to talk like normal human beings, with their mouths.

As if guided by the same persistent celestial spirit, he led her outside the courtyard and up a spiral staircase until they were alone on a balcony above the hedges and fountains that lay, not surprisingly, below. He held her in his strong, sinewy arms, the spyglass in his belt making a dent in her Person, but she felt nothing as Love had anesthetized her.

He spoke directly to her for the first time with his mouth: "Surely you are an apparition of the night," he said, his voice as handsome and dashing as he himself was. "I feel as if I have drifted into a glorious sleep and you are my dream, my lovely dream."

"Behold . . . how the moonlight . . . plays upon the splashing waters," she said coyly, reciting a phrase she had read in a romantic novel. Obediently, he glanced toward the garden but saw no splashing waters there, as the fountain had been shut off.

"Are we sleepwalkers in someone's bewitching nocturnal fantasies?" he continued. "Are we the figments of some divine poet's imagination, with you the verse and me the stanza?" He was clearly on a roll now. "I have never felt my heartstrings pulled so sharply as they are being pulled at this moment. I feel as if they will snap, and my heart will be flung across the garden into yonder lake."

Vanessa glanced at the lake and felt vaguely queasy at the thought of her Loved One's heart, arteries adrift, floating along the surface.

"But who *are* you, beautiful apparition?" the stranger inquired handsomely. "Why have I never seen you before here or elsewhere?"

Vanessa knitted her perfect brow over this one. What could she tell him that would at once intrigue him yet not betray her father's command, thus unleashing her sisters' heinous wrath? What sweet-scented response could she make that would convey the true intensity of her feelings yet remain mysteriously veiled?

"Beats me," she said.

"Then will you not at least remove your mask? Will you not, for the love of all that is holy, show me what I cannot but express the tenderest feelings for?"

"I cannot . . . I dare not . . . it would not be proper . . . or right . . . for two people on such short acquaintance . . . to be so bold . . . with each other." Vanessa had a tendency, when in the grip of rapture, to speak in dots. "On the other hand . . . why not?" she said. Vanessa also had a tendency to change her mind impulsively. Swiftly, she reached up and took off her mask.

Immediately, the stranger gripped his heart, for her

Beauty was truly arresting, in the cardiac sense. Though neither of them spoke, somehow she knew that he knew who she was, and he knew that she knew that he knew who she was. It was somewhat confusing, but it was the language of love.

"I love you," he said, taking her face in his firm hand and caressing her cheek as if it were the bud of a flower. He pulled her tightly to him again and she knew, inevitably, as the earth seems to know when Spring is about to burst in early September, that she was about to be . . . kissed. But first . . .

She gave a little cry of protest.

"Sir! You, too, must remove your mask! I showed you mine, now you must show me yours!"

"Ha-hah!" he exclaimed, the gently teasing lilt returning to his voice. "What if I do not?"

She gave a little cry of delight.

"Then I shall have to peel it off!"

"Will you now, my little pretty?"

Now *this* was what romance was all about.

"That I will, my large handsome," she said.

"Are you so certain, my little bluebell?"

"Indeed I am, my big azalea."

After a few more quips of a horticultural nature, she grew impatient.

"Please!" she cried. "Remove your mask, too, sir, that I may gaze upon your unfettered features!"

Giving in, the stranger raised a strong, bronzed hand to his finely chiseled face and took the edge of his mask. With one tug, the mask would be off and Vanessa would be gazing into the face of the man she would adore forever more. That is, assuming he was cute.

As his hand gripped the mask tightly . . . the garden door crashed open with a loud clang!

30

There, breathing heavily, were two figures: an angry bloodhound and a livid rooster. Vanessa keenly identified them as being her father and her escort, Lord Gastleigh. Before the love-struck Vanessa could utter either a word or a dot, her father had pulled her away from her would-be lover with a force that seemed unusual for an elderly rooster. At the same time, Lord Gastleigh had shoved the stranger rudely away.

"Unpaw me, sir!" the stranger demanded of Lord Gastleigh. "I demand to know the meaning of this intrusion upon my Person!"

"You, sir, are a scoundrel!" Lord Gastleigh barked.

"A fiend!" crowed her father.

"But father—" Vanessa protested vainly.

At that moment, since he had no gauntlet, Lord Gastleigh threw his detachable paw at the stranger's face. "I demand satisfaction!" he declared.

"Am I to interpret this as a challenge to a duel?" the stranger asked, grasping the situation quickly.

"Indeed you are!"

"Then choose your weapon!" said the stranger bravely.

Lord Gastleigh began to howl derisively. "He doesn't even know the elementary rules of dueling and killing!" he said to the old Duke and to Vanessa, slapping his hind legs. "It's you, as the challenged party, who gets to choose weapons!"

"Dueling swords," said the stranger nonchalantly. "Name the day."

"On the morrow, at dusk," said Lord Gastleigh.

"The morrow?" asked the stranger. "Oh, sorry, that's already booked. I have a previous challenge at that time."

"Tuesday at dawn, then," said Lord Gastleigh, a little taken aback.

The stranger took a small leather book from his breast pocket and began leafing through the pages, wetting his handsome index finger as he did so. "Let me see," he said. "Tuesday dawn I fight the Lord of Flatbush . . . Tuesday dusk I do battle with the Duke of Hazzard . . . Wednesday dawn I take on a Prince of a Guy . . . Wednesday dusk is—"

"Well, can you fit me in on the twenty-third?" sputtered Lord Gastleigh impatiently. "That's a fortnight hence."

"Hence it is," the stranger said in agreement, writing down his newest opponent's name with a clip-on quill he carried expressly for the purpose.

Vanessa's father has been watching the exchange with keen interest, his coxcomb flapping lightly in the breeze. He spoke with measured cadence:

"Mark my words. You shall never again see my daughter. Never, as long as I live or breathe!"

"But father—" Vanessa cried out.

"Hush your face!" said the old Duke. "Come with me at once! We will hie hither from this place hence!"

And without another word, he took Vanessa under his wing and dragged her off to her destiny.

BOOK II

Fate Turns About Again

♡   ♡   ♡

It seemeth poor consolation when romance is in flower
To consider that love departeth every hour on the hour.
Andrew Herring, 1817

Chapter
4

♡   ♡   ♡

Alone in the clattering carriage with her father, Vanessa wept bitter tears, which rolled down her rosy cheeks and fell upon her crimson gown, moistening it. The driver, at the orders of her father, the kindly old Duke, was lashing the horses with a vengeance, though a whip would have been more practical. Through her tears, she could see that her father, whose rooster head rested on the seat between them, was still flushed with anger.

"You must never, ever see that scoundrel again," he said quietly but firmly, giving his own forehead a smack of the riding crop for emphasis. "Otherwise I will be forced to take the harshest measures."

"But . . . why?" Vanessa sobbed ardently.

Her father said nothing and gazed stolidly out the carriage window. For a moment, there was no sound but the whinny of the horses and the *thwack!* of the riding crop against the old Duke's aristocratic forehead.

"Is it because . . . I did not await Lord Gastleigh dutifully when he went to . . . wash up?" Vanessa also tended to speak in dots when she was in the grip of romantic misery.

The kindly old Duke said nothing.

"Nothing," he said.

"Is it because . . . the stranger took too many . . . liberties?"

Again, there was no response.

"Is it because . . . he is a bounder and a rake?"

Still no answer. Vanessa was running low on reasons.

"Please Father," she beseeched him. "There must be some explanation for your extreme displeasure. Could it . . . might it . . . possibly be because . . . he is . . . the Duke . . . of Earl?"

It was just a wild guess, a musket shot in the dark, but the look on her father's face told her the guess had hit home.

"You're getting warmer," the kindly old Duke said grudgingly.

"Oh, Father!" she cried with relief. "If that is all it is! I know about his reputation already! I am no longer a child! I know he is a cad, a scoundrel, a rake, and a hoe!"

"A hoe?"

"Never mind," Vanessa said, touched by her father's concern for that most precious, that most sacrosanct of a young woman's attributes—her purity.

"Dear, dear Papa," she said, smiling through her tears. "Do not be afraid that I would . . . give in . . . to his romantic wiles. I am not like the other girls who have . . . fallen prey . . . to his charms. And besides"—her rapture edged up a notch—"he loves me and . . . I love him!"

At this, the kindly old Duke sat upright and his eyes flashed with an anger and determination Vanessa had never beheld before.

"No!" he shouted. "You will never, never see each other

again!" There was spittle on his kindly old mouth. "Never while I am still alive! Never!"

Again, Vanessa broke into sobs. How could her father be so unreasonable? How could he speak to her thus? What was the big deal?

"But why, Father?" she beseeched him. "Just tell me why, I beg of you!"

The kindly old Duke felt that his heart might melt, but realized it would be messy at best. Still, he was clearly moved by her sincere perplexity. He spoke more calmly.

"It is not for any of the reasons you mentioned that I oppose your love for this—this blackguard," he said. "It is because of a solemn promise I made to your dear departed mother upon her demise."

"My mother?" Vanessa asked, with yet more sincere perplexity. "What pray tell, does Mama have to do with this dilemma?"

The kindly old Duke took a deep breath and considered his next words carefully.

"When your mother was dying," he said, "I went to her deathbed, as is the custom. She gripped my hand and with her dying breath asked me to promise her two things. One of the things I solemnly promised was that I would never, ever reveal the deep, dark, tragic secret pertaining to you, dear daughter—and to the young Duke of Earl."

"What deep, dark, tragic secret, Papa?"

"I cannot tell you, though I wish I could," the kindly old Duke said. "I made a solemn oath on your mother's deathbed, and those are the best kind."

"Then what about the other promise?" Vanessa asked. "What was the other promise?"

"That I would see to having the drapes cleaned," the kindly old Duke said.

"But Papa—"

"Already I have told you too much, daughter. From now on my lips are sealed on the subject. I pray you not to ever bring it up to me again as long as I'm alive. You will *never* see the Duke of Earl again. That is all."

So for the rest of the journey they sat silent, the Duke having dabbed some sealing wax on his lips. Only the sound of the horses' whinnying was heard, as the driver laid his whip onto their backs. They were not the only creatures suffering that night.

♡   ♡   ♡

Back at the family castle, Vanessa retired to her room, donned her rags, and lay in bed for a week, quietly weeping to herself. She wept until her poor tear ducts could no longer produce the required fluid so necessary for weepage.

At night, she tossed and turned in bed, tormented by the terrible, unthinkable thought that she could never see her One True Love again. Half aslumber, she would experience the same odd dream night after night.

In this nocturnal reverie, a terrible storm was always raging outside, the usual place for storms. Thunder would roll, lightning would crackle fiercely, and rain would pour down like some waterfall from the Great Beyond. Suddenly, in the flash of a lightning bolt, she would see her Lover outside on her balcony, having leapt up dashingly twenty feet from the ground below. Rising, she would go to the window, give her Lover a smile as beautiful as life itself, and gesture with her hand that he was to wait until she made herself more beautiful for him. She would then sweetly draw the curtains as he awaited on the balcony amidst the raging storm.

In her dream she would then get into a tub and bathe herself with sweet-smelling oils and other petroleum products, then sprinkle a soft talc over every inch of her near-perfect anatomy. Following this, she would daub fine French perfume from Barcelona behind each earlobe, then place a necklace of pearls about her swan-white nape. Next, she would slowly brush her hair 560 strokes, as was her custom, and apply mascara, lipstick, rouge, and a beauty spot. She would pluck her eyebrows sensuously, then put up her tresses in a fashionable beehive hairdo.

Another loud thunderclap could be heard in the eastern sky, but it would not deter Vanessa from the refinement of her Beauty. For Beauty was something she possessed in a way that few had ever possessed it before—as has been stated on several occasions. Meanwhile, she would hear a thumping on her windowpane, and smile, knowing it was her Lover, impatient to enter her boudoir and declare his undying love for her. How impetuous he was! Imagine, wanting to enter her bedchamber before she had even had a chance to paint her nails! Why, she still had to put on five ruffled petticoats, choose the appropriate gown for the occasion, and consider what shoes she would slip onto her small, dainty, perfectly proportioned feet. Then, and only then, would it be right to meet her One True Love!

When at last she was ready, she would unlatch the balcony window and let her Lover in. Three-quarters drowned, he would stumble into the room, his skin wrinkled, his feet squishing, and wring out his hair, pour water from his various pockets, release the burgeoning tidewaters that had formed in his shoes, and scrub off the rust that had begun to form on his sword. Then he would finally approach her, water dripping from his nose, and take her in his arms. But just as they were going to bring their lips together, as was customary for the successful execution of a kiss, the sound of her father's footsteps would be heard on the stairs. Alas, their clandestine meeting would come to a swift and frustrating end. Her Lover would hie himself hence from her bedchamber and thence into the stormy night whence he had come.

And there the reverie would end. A tragic dream befitting a tragic love!

♡   ♡   ♡

On the seventh morning of Vanessa's convalescence, a strange thing happened. Brigitte, her lady-in-waiting, was busy performing her main tasks, which consisted largely of waiting in various places. Of course, she had tried to bring her mistress pots of steaming potato tea, which she said was used to cure melancholia in the French provinces, but Vanessa had been too wan to drink any. This morning, Brigitte was waiting somewhat more impatiently than usual outside Vanessa's bedchamber while the kindly old Duke completed his morning visit. After the lord of the manor had departed, Brigitte entered quietly and stood before her mistress as the morning sun poured in through the windows.

"Bon soiree," said she. "Oy was in the village this mornin', missy, and a gen'man, tall and 'ansome 'e was, give me this." Brigitte handed Vanessa a small envelope, sealed and embossed with a noble crest—a glorious eagle's head with a somewhat more puzzling mouse's tail hanging from its beak.

"'E tole me to deliver it to my mistress *toot sweet,*" Brigitte continued, "but not to tell a soul about it. I did a fine curtsy and tole the gen'man, *'Bye-en sewer,* Your Grace. And 'e was off."

"Merci, buttercups et alouette," Vanessa said fluently but

crisply, her mind already on the contents of the envelope. She bade her lady-in-waiting wait outside.

Alone, Vanessa fondled the envelope in her hands, studying it intently before opening the seal. As she did so, her heart raced, though it did not win, place, or show. Deep down, she knew from whom the note was sent, though she did not know what the message was. For that, she well knew, she would have to read it.

Ripping open the crested seal, she devoured the page as hungrily as if she were a starving woman. There, in strong, virile penmanship, was the message from her One True Love:

> Dearest,
>
> I cannot bare my eggsistence without seeing you agin. Pleez make ebery effort to make a ~~rondez-randy rindesvo~~ meeting this afternoon at three o' the clok at Ye Olde Composte Heape.
>
> My love for you is ~~magnafi stoopend~~ big.
>
> Pleez accept my destingished sintements.
>
> Yours as long as I live or the sun cantinues to rise, whadever comes first . . .
>
> Signed,
>
> A. A.   ☺
>
> Anthony Ardent
> Duke of Earl

Vanessa placed the precious note to her heaving but modest breast, and for the first time in half a fortnight, she smiled. A glorious, beaming smile! It was such a forceful, virile note, even if his spelling was atrocious. Now she remembered the story: The young Duke of Earl, it was said, had been expelled from Eton before finishing his English courses because of an affair of honor involving the wife of the don, an Italian-born gentleman named Corleone. Wasn't that just like the scoundrel? Vanessa thought. But what was a little wretched spelling between two lovers as destined for love as they? Hoping she could decipher the note, she read it again and again, her heart fluttering when she got one after another of the misspellings right and finally figured out the terrible, thrilling truth: Her One True Love wanted to meet her at Ye Olde Composte Heape at three this very afternoon! Heavens, that was barely an hour away!

Immediately, or shortly thereafter, the reality of the situation dawned on Vanessa. How could she meet her own sweet Anthony, the Duke of Earl, when her father had expressly forbidden her to ever see him again? She had never, ever disobeyed her father's commands, even when it was obvious he was quite addled.

Yet this time something stronger tugged at her heart, guiding her to the knowledge that she must defy her beloved father and hie to her Lover. Was it her own indomitable will that compelled her thus? Was it the bond, as yet unbroken, that had been forged between them? Or was that celestial spirit still hanging around?

Quietly, as if in a dream, Vanessa prepared her body as rapidly as possible for the forthcoming rendezvous. She ministered to her exquisite anatomy for about forty-five minutes, stared at her supple, sensuous, etc. body in the mirror for several more minutes, then donned the one dress she had saved in a hope chest expressly for such a rendezvous—a burlap gown with a dainty lace along the hem.

She hoped she would be able to sneak past her father on her way down the stairs, since the kindly old Duke spent much of his waking hours asleep by the fireside. But as she descended the stairs with the grace and elegance that were her birthright, she suddenly heard the *thwack!* of a scepter against a noble forehead. Her father was alert! As she passed the study door, he called out to her.

"Why, daughter! Have you ceased your sniveling, my dearest?"

"Indeed I have, Papa," said Vanessa sweetly. "I am feeling so much better I thought I would take my horse for a ride. Indeed, I may even get upon him."

"Excellent, excellent," said the kindly old Duke. "I knew a few days of wailing and teeth-gnashing would cure you of these feelings you say you have for the Earl boy."

"As always, Father, you were right," said Vanessa, nearly choking on the words. For her natural virtue and truthfulness, as much a part of her as her Beauty, rebelled against the lie she was now telling. But this was Love that impelled her, True Love, so what could she do?

Vanessa strode purposefully toward the Sherwin-Williams stables to choose her favorite steed, a white Arabian stallion named Muammar Farouk El-Fezzi. With one swift kick of her tiny, perfect heels against the stallion's straining sides, they were off, galloping across the sylvan bog and mottled heathrow. Just past the most mottled part of the heathrow was the castle graveyard, where generations of Sherwin-Williamses had been buried. She often visited her mother's grave there, leaving flowers and chocolates by the tombstone. But this time she and Muammar Farouk El-Fezzi were riding with the wind, so she tarried not.

With the speed of a desert sandstorm, they had arrived at Ye Olde Composte Heape, and Vanessa tethered Muammar

Farouk El-Fezzi to a tree. She stood by the steaming heapage, her tresses blowing behind her from the force of the pungent breeze, a silhouette of loveliness in the afternoon. Even from afar, it would have been obvious that this was a woman awaiting her One True Love.

He appeared, as if out of a mist, from behind a steaming mound. His bronzed and chiseled face, now without a mask, was as handsome as she had ever dared to hope. She could see his flinty grey eyes, which straddled a fine, aquiline nose, which was itself set firmly above a gentle yet cruel mouth, located just north of a manly jutting chin, set firmly upon a strong, muscular neck, and so forth. Without a word, they drew near, and he gathered her in two of his strong and bronzed arms. Their lips locked in a tempestuous kiss.

"Oh, my Duke . . . my Anthony . . ." she moaned.

"Call me Tony," he moaned back. "How I have pined for your touch! How I have oaked for your embrace!"

"If this . . . be not love . . . I . . . do not know . . . what . . . might . . . be," Vanessa said, her dots running amuck.

"'Tis truly love, my dearest," he averred. "'Tis love on a higher plane than what was felt by the gods of ancient Greece." Once again, their lips came together and for the first time Vanessa opened her mouth. Letting her tongue loose from its moorings, she searched his handsome mouth, then explored his fine front teeth, between which she noted a small particle of food, probably bacon. With a slight gasp, she pulled gently away from him.

"My father has vowed to punish me gravely if ever we were to meet again," she said, having remembered the kindly old Duke's threats.

"But why?" her Lover asked. "I know I do not possess the most unsullied reputation in Devonshire. But in my love for you, all is different, all is pure. Surely the world, or at least the county, must know that by now."

Vanessa gave a little cry of passion.

"Oh, yes, my love. But it is not your reputation, depraved though it may be, that threatens to separate us for eternity and beyond."

"Then what's up?" the Duke of Earl asked, sincerely perplexed.

"I do not know exactly," Vanessa said. "It is most mysterious. My father claims he made a certain deathbed vow to my dying mother. It concerned both you and me—though how that could be, I know not."

A silence replaced the quiet that had prevailed during their meeting of love. The Duke's face went from a healthy, ruddy complexion to a deathly white. He stood stock-still, with a slight tremor coursing down the length of his body. It was clear that something had occurred to him.

"Could it be?" he said, almost to himself. "Could it possibly be?" He said a bit louder. "Could it, by any stretch of the most terrifying imagination, possibly *be*?" The young Duke was winding himself up again for another good one. "Is it conceivable, by the heavens above or the inferno below, that by some unthinkable—"

"Could we cut to the chase, my dearest?" Vanessa asked not unkindly.

The Duke of Earl looked down at his Love, cupped her chin again as if it were the most delicate of roses, and said, with the saddest voice she had ever heard:

"I *may* know something. But it will be tragic for both of us should even part of the truth be true."

Vanessa looked up at him and braced herself. Something told her that what was about to happen in the next several minutes would affect her life, her love, her destiny.

Chapter

5

♡   ♡   ♡

"Once, many years ago, when I was a child," the Duke of Earl began, "I happened to overhear two of my dear departed father's maids gossiping in the garden. They were witches, those two, always trading evil tales about others. I had been hiding in a hedge, one of my favorite childhood pastimes."

Vanessa listened, her heart picking up speed once again. She almost didn't want to hear what her Loved One had to say, but knew that she must.

"What did they say?" she inquired in a quavering voice.

"It was most likely just evil rumors, but I remember something that struck me even at that age," he said. He continued tentatively. "It concerned my father . . . and . . . your own late mother."

"My mother was *never* tardy!" Vanessa exclaimed loyally.

"Pardon me," the young Duke apologized. "I meant it in the dead sense."

"Oh," said Vanessa. "Go on, please."

"According to this infamous rumor, my father and your mother were . . . intimate." He paused while Vanessa blushed deeply. "They supposedly had an affair that lasted many years and that"—the young Duke took a long breath—"produced a child. Following the birth of that child, they both . . . were supposed to have . . . committed suicide . . . together!"

It was simply too much. Vanessa refused even to believe her One True Love had spoken, much less that he had spoken thusly about her mother. She shook her beautiful hair slowly, the steam from the compost mingling lightly in the russet tresses. Then, suddenly, anger welled up in her shapely yet modest bosom. Her fiery, loyal nature asserted itself like a lioness protecting her pride.

"How dare you besmirch the name of my dear mother with those terrible words!" she cried.

"But I was only saying what I recalled—"

"You are a cad!" Vanessa shouted, suddenly hating him. "You are a blackguard, a scoundrel, a rake, and a hoe!"

"A hoe?"

"Never mind!" she exclaimed. "I despise you! You are no gentleman, sir! No proper gentleman would breathe such vile lies to a lady!" At that, no longer able to contain her anger, Vanessa slapped the young Duke across the cheek with her soft yet hard hand.

Stunned by her fiery outburst, he stood speechless as she continued her passionate and tempestuous tirade. "My father was right!" she cried, almost against the restraints of her yearning heart. "You are a bounder! We will never see each other again, much less date! I would not see you, sir, if you were the last man on earth! I hope Lord Gastleigh makes an end to you during your duel a week hence!"

"A fortnight," the young Duke corrected her quietly.

"Whatever," said Vanessa. With that, Vanessa gathered up

her burlap skirts and jumped upon her waiting steed, the faithful Muammar Farouk El-Fezzi. With a sharp kick from her beautifully rounded heels, horse and rider were off in a flurry of compost clods, headed toward the Sherwin-Williams Castle. Left behind was the young Duke of Earl, for once the jilted one, but in this case mourning the loss of his One True Love with a perplexity that was tragically sincere.

♡   ♡   ♡

Brokenhearted, infuriated, and incredibly miffed, Vanessa kept her dashing steed at a frantic gallop across the glade and heathrow, wind whipping through her hair, gnats splattering against her forehead. Muammar Farouk El-Fezzi sped across the sylvan bogs and speckled glades like a white bolt of lightning, his eager nostrils flaring, his strong legs agallop in a blur of motion.

They sped along the edge of the tall palisades that ringed the county of Devonshire, falling sharply to the sea. Named after a faithful canine retainer of one of Vanessa's ancestors, the rocky promontory was known as the Cliffs of Rover. Though preoccupied with her own ire, Vanessa could not help but notice a gaunt figure standing at the edge of the cliffs, silhouetted against the darkening sky. She could just hear the man moaning, "Oh, Jane, my Jane!" She realized at once it was the *other* county character, Rochester, who had recently taken up with his housekeeper, plain-looking Miss Eyre. Really! What was this county coming to! Through clenched but ruby-red lips, Vanessa murmured to herself that the county authorities should do something about these romantic chaps, forever wandering about wailing.

Meanwhile, she had her own romantic dilemma to consider. As she thought about the terrible events that had just transpired, tears of anger and frustration poured down her peach-clear cheeks. What a vile cad he was! What a thoughtless bounder! How could she have fallen in love with one such as he? To even utter such horrid lies was more than wounding—what was worse, it suggested improper breeding. To besmirch the hallowed name of her poor, dear mother was . . . beyond forgiveness. No, she would never again think of him, much less remember her deep and abiding love for him.

Yet Vanessa was a fiery creature of impetuousness, and no sooner had these thoughts put in an appearance than she changed her mind; it was, after all, a lady's prerogative. For she admitted at once that, deep down, in the very essence of her Being, she still loved the young Duke as she had never loved anyone before. On the other hand, she thought, instantly changing her mind yet again, he was the most horrible man she had ever known, and she hated him! It was all getting out of hand. Perhaps it would become clearer once she got back to her lady-in-waiting, Brigitte, who would calm her nerves with a small snifter of potato absinthe.

Though she had vowed not to give the vile insinuations of her ex-One True Love even the dignity of her attentions, she could not prevent herself from thinking of them. Of course they were lies, contrived by two horrible rumormongers to besmirch the good names of Ardent and Sherwin-Williams. But no matter how hard she tried, the horrifying implications kept stealing into her mind.

Absurd! If, as he had suggested, her mother had been . . . indelicate . . . with the young Duke's father, their child would be a . . . bastard! Her blood ran cold at the thought. Even more than that, she thought, the little bastard might well be . . . the young Duke! Her blood ran colder. Or . . . Or . . . the child might be none other than Vanessa herself! Her blood froze.

Though it was hardly ladylike, she waved her arms in circles and flapped her legs up and down in the stirrups to return her blood to a lukewarm state. Heavens above! The possibilities were terrifying! It would mean, at the very least, that she and her hated, beloved Anthony Ardent, the eighth Duke of Earl, were in fact half brother and half sister!

No! A thousand times no! It was impossible! Why, they didn't even look alike! He had short hair; she had long hair! He wore long pants; she wore gowns! Impossible! She vowed to rid herself of the disgusting thoughts permeating her pristine mind. Best not even to think about it. She would think about Love and Beauty instead.

But hark! There was one small detail of the witches' tale that kept intruding into her mind, tormenting her. It was the claim that her mother and the young Duke's father had committed suicide . . . together! How unthinkable! But if . . . they had . . . then wouldn't it stand to reason that . . . that . . .

Suddenly, Vanessa was gripped by an idea, her first in several chapters. Yes, she thought, it would put to rest this hateful lie once and for all! It was the very essence of simplicity: Because she had dutifully visited her mother's grave so often, she had memorized every word on her dear departed mother's tombstone. As she rode with the wind and the gnats, she recalled the inscription: "Here lieth Lady Hepsibah Sherwin-Williams. Born December 3, 1807. Died June 23, 1841. No Comment."

These poetic sentiments had always made her cry, and she wept now as she turned her faithful white steed around and raced in the opposite direction whence she had come. Her destination: the cemetery where many of the Duke of Earl's departed ones lay buried, many of them underground.

The sky was dark and eerie above her as she flew down the highway. Vanessa could not repress a shiver as she saw the

Silhouettes of swaying branches casting shadows like mad Harlequins dancing on the cobblestones below. Goodness, was it any *wonder* that this part of the county seemed so romantic? Although the billowing clouds above seemed to glower at her like huge bushy eyebrows, as if forewarning her, Vanessa felt that her need to know the dark and tragic secret was stronger than any mere mortal dread.

Arriving at the cemetery, Vanessa gave a final shiver and dismounted bravely, tying Muammar Farouk El-Fezzi to one of the skinnier tombstones that loomed before her. Slowly she went from grave to grave, peering at the weathered headstones, thinking deep thoughts about life and death and such. As she deciphered the faint wording of various epitaphs, she paused momentarily at one headstone, which read, simply, "I Didst *Tell* Thee I Was Ill," and moved on.

Suddenly Vanessa found the one she was looking for. She stopped in her tracks, then stepped out of them. Her heart began to pound louder than it ever had before. She read the epitaph once quickly, then once slowly. When she had taken in the full meaning of the gravestone, she clasped her hand to her thumping heart, fell abruptly to her knees, and fainted away in an all-out swoon.

The stone read: "Here lieth Mortimer Ardent, Seventh Duke of Earl. Born November 4, 1801. Died June 23, 1841. Don't Ask."

♡ ♡ ♡

Vanessa lay afaint in the dark and muddy graveyard until dusk, at which time she was awakened by the hoot of a confused lark. Barely able to recall where she was or why she was here, Vanessa picked herself up, dusted herself off, and started all over again. In a kind of trance, she mounted her trusty steed and began her weary ride home.

Trotting along in the gathering twilight, Vanessa tried to piece together all she had heard and seen this eventful afternoon. Could it be true? Could the awfulness of what she had discovered be as awful as it seemed? Or was there a chance it was merely some tragic coincidence? Surely . . . she thought, lapsing into dots, she could not be . . . the . . . dare she think it? . . . illegitimate daughter of the Duke of Earl, Senior, and . . . her beloved mother? No, it was impossible! That would make her father—her *supposed* father, she choked—Lord Sherwin-Williams, a . . . a . . . cuckold! And would that not explain his uncharacteristic anger over her tryst with the young Duke at the ball? No! Ten thousand times no! It was nothing more than a horrible series of coincidences!

Her faithful steed chose that moment to snort loudly. To her delicate and smoothly shaped ears, it sounded like the horse was whinnying "Fat chance!"

Back at the stables, she handed the reins of Muammar Farouk El-Fezzi to the stable boy and stumbled up the path to the castle. Opening the massive oak door, she walked quietly in, but was surprised to see her father pacing up and down the parlor, swatting himself on the forehead with the scepter at an alarming rate. Tired, dirty, and disillusioned, Vanessa tried to sneak past the parlor door, but she was unsuccessful.

"Dearest daughter!" came a thin bellow. "Come hither this instant!"

Obediently, Vanessa entered the Great Parlour, trying to hide the mud and dirt on her burlap dress. "Yes, Papa," she said as meekly as possible, repressing her fiery and tempestuous nature for the moment.

"Where have you been, daughter?" the kindly old Duke asked in a voice laden with firm resolve.

"Been?"

"Yes. I demand an answer as I am your father, as you doubtless know."

Something inside Vanessa shivered at this unintended example of what Brigitte might refer to as a *double antandry*. How perfectly ironic, she thought.

"I have been out, Papa," she said simply.

"I deduced that from the fact that it was necessary for you to pass through the front door in order to get *in*," the old man said with a trace of impatience. "Had you already been in, this effort would have been needless. Now Vanessa, I shall ask you only once again: where have you *been*?"

"At Ye Olde Composte Heape," she admitted.

"And what was the purpose of this visit?"

"To view the compost," Vanessa fibbed. "I have always been fascinated by compost and the heapage thereof."

Exasperated, the kindly old Duke produced a piece of paper from his breast pocket and waved it about. Vanessa recognized it as her ex-Lover's note. "Did you go to Ye Olde Composte Heape with that illiterate scoundrel?"

"Which scoundrel, Papa?"

"How many scoundrels do you know, girl?" the old man fairly shouted. "Especially one with the spelling skill of a partridge?"

"You mean Anthony Ardent, the Duke of Earl?" she said in a whisper.

"Of course I do."

"Yes," she admitted. "I met him. But—"

"That will be all, daughter. I will abide none of your explanations. You have defied my orders, lied to me, and gotten compost on your dress. As promised, you will be punished."

At this point, Vanessa was standing with her head bowed. Despite her fiery and unpredictable nature, she stood ready to take her punishment stoically, without complaint. That was the kind of woman she was: She would take it calmly and without a sound.

"I have decided to send you away for an indefinite period of time," said the old Duke.

Vanessa shrieked, shattering a priceless crystal on the mantelpiece.

"Yes," said the kindly old Duke, barely perturbed. "You will be dispatched hence as soon as possible to Auntie Bellum and Uncle Ravenel in far-off New Orleans. I will make the arrangements on the morrow and you will depart within the fortnight!"

"But Papa—"

"I will not hear another word," the old man said, covering his ears. "You have obviously been rolling around in the compost with this . . . this bounder! You have thus shamed the name of Sherwin-Williams and your various and sundry forebears. Good night, my daughter!"

With that, the elderly scion marched off to his study, leaving poor Vanessa alone in the Great Parlour. After a moment's time she heard the familiar *thwack!* and hied herself up to her bedchamber. It was a long walk up the polished stairway, and in a daze, Vanessa wondered if it would be the last time she would make this climb. She wondered with a catch in her heart if her destiny awaited her at the top of this stairway and beyond.

But it was not her destiny that awaited her. It was her lady-in-waiting.

"Ow bout some nice potato cocoa, moydmezelle?" asked Brigitte.

Chapter

6

♡   ♡   ♡

*C*onfined to her bedchamber until preparations could be made for her imminent journey to the New World, Vanessa stood by her window every night and beseeched the heavens for some answer to her tragic dilemma. Was she really the illegitimate daughter of the departed Duke of Earl and her equally departed mother? Had they really committed suicide together out of shame? Was her ex-One True Love, the young Duke of Earl, really her half brother? Was anybody following any of this? And finally, did her father really think the Duke of Earl had compromised her—dare she utter the thought?—her chastity? So many questions entered her mind. So few answers exited.

During the long days of confinement, she was visited only by Brigitte, who attended her with typical Gallic loyalty, and by her three sisters, who stopped by one at a time to utter a consoling word or two about her grievous fate.

"Most likely, you will be kidnapped by pirates and sold into white slavery," consoled Lady Gertrude. "You will probably

be pillaged, plundered and left to die on an island somewhere."
Gertrude was jumping up and down in sympathy.

"You'll probably perish from the ocean voyage," Lady
Agnes said, beaming in consolation. "If the sailors don't lash you
to death while you're stripped to the waist"—here Lady Agnes
could not repress a whoop of sympathy—"the scurvy will probably get you!"

But it was Lady Ralph whose consolation made the greatest
impact on Vanessa: "The sea air will just *ruin* your nails," she
rasped. Vanessa, ever conscious of the effect of the elements
upon her Person, was left by her three sisters to contemplate this
terrible prospect.

Alas, there were other terrible prospects to contemplate as
well: For instance, why had she heard nothing from her ex-One
True Love? Surely her declaration of loathing for him, her
smacking him in the face, and the possibility that they were
brother and sister should not discourage True Romance! At the
very least, she might have expected a note, no matter how badly
spelled, to tell her how he proposed to dispatch Lord Gastleigh
in the upcoming duel.

All these thoughts were interrupted suddenly one afternoon by the entrance of Brigitte, who was bringing Vanessa
tidings and lunch, both of which made her nauseous.

"You're to pack all your clothes, moydmezelle," said the
lady-in-waiting to her beloved mistress. "We're to leave on the
morrow at dawn's early light!" She began to hum cheerfully.

"*We?*" Vanessa asked.

"Oui, we," Brigitte replied.

"Are you saying *oui* or we, Brigitte?"

"Oui, we, milady. *Oui,* we."

Vanessa sighed heavily at her handmaiden's dimness. The
French! "Do you mean the *oui* of your native tongue or the
English meaning—we as in us?"

"Oui."

"O-u-i or w-e?" Vanessa asked in exasperation.

"Oui, we," Brigitte declared happily. *"Oui,* we!"

"Don't be crude," Vanessa said. As a woman of breeding, she did not tolerate chamber-pot humor.

Later, however, Brigitte returned to explain in somewhat more comprehensible terms the details of Vanessa's impending voyage. As it was the peak tourist season, the old Duke had been unable to secure passage on one of the prestigious ocean liners and had opted instead for no-frills accommodations on the HMS *Sir Freddie,* a merchant vessel carrying a cargo of textiles and European diseases to the New World. The vessel was scheduled to depart on the morrow at half-past dawn, sharp, and would arrive in New Orleans two weeks hence.

"And Oy'm to be your chaperony," said Brigitte excitedly. "Your papa's instructed me never to leave you alone come hell or high water."

"Tell my father I must see him before we depart," Vanessa ordered.

"His dukeship don't wish to see you, moydmezelle," Brigitte reported. "He says he'll see you in 'bout two years, when you return with a better attitude to marry your Intended."

At the words *marry, Intended,* and *the,* Vanessa's heart jumped, then hopped and skipped a bit. At least they were back into her field of expertise. "Did . . . did . . . he mention anyone . . . in particular?"

"Lord Gastleigh," she said, "if he survives the duel. In the meantime, Oy'm to make sure you remain chased, though Oy dunno by who."

At that, the wellsprings holding back the floodwaters of the tidal wave of tears broke in Vanessa, and she wept uncontrollably. As her lady-in-waiting packed her steamer trunk, Vanessa wept for her lost love, for her father's lack of understanding, for the prospect of a disastrous betrothal to a man she despised, and for the fact that her fingernails would never be the same. It was all too much, and Vanessa was not sure she would live through it.

♡ ♡ ♡

Unaccustomed to ocean voyages—this being her first—Vanessa became intensely seasick before the HMS *Sir Freddie* had left the dock. It became even worse once she actually boarded the ship and was shown to her stateroom, a small, cramped cabin to be shared by the *Sir Freddie*'s three paying passengers—Vanessa, Brigitte and a free-lance Gypsy named Rose Leigh. The Gypsy, it turned out, was traveling to the New World to read palms and tell fortunes, as there was a severe shortage of seers there.

Though the Gypsy at least promised to be an interesting companion, Vanessa began to perceive that her biggest problem was going to be Brigitte. The idiotic girl insisted on interpreting the kindly old Duke's instructions literally and would not let Vanessa out of her sight for a second.

"Really, Brigitte," Vanessa said one stormy afternoon. "I think it's hardly necessary for you to accompany me to the side of the ship every time I feel unease come upon my Person."

"Oy promised *votre pear* Oy'd follow ye everywheres," Brigitte said dutifully, "though Oy'd 'preciate it if ye'd *barfe* downwind next time. Oy only brought three dresses."

"*Barfe?*" Vanessa asked. "What, pray tell, is *barfe?*"

" 'Tis French," the maid translated, "for toss votre cookies."

And so it went for the next fortnight. In the evening, Vanessa would lie awake into the night listening to the Gypsy, Rose Leigh, tell stories about her ribald past. Naturally, Vanessa was too virtuous to listen to such talk and would chastely cover her ears with her hands, uncovering them only for the good parts.

On afternoons when the sea was calm, Rose Leigh would sit with Vanessa and Brigitte and practice telling their fortunes.

"Let's see, Brigitte," she would say, studying the maid's ruddy palm. "Yer from France, right?" Brigitte nodded. "Now I'm thinking of a particular part of France—would it be . . . Sicily?"

"Faith an' begorrah," Brigitte exclaimed. "You're right!" It was indeed amazing, all three women agreed, that she had been able to pick out the maiden's home province. Then Rose turned her attention to Vanessa and picked up her slender, soft, supple hand and turned it palm up. Unsurprisingly, Vanessa's palm was flawless, without a single line upon it.

"This is truly a beautiful palm," said the Gypsy perceptively. "And it tells your complete history. Let's see: Your father is a leather tanner"—she looked up to Vanessa for confirmation, but found none—"no, no, I misspeak myself. He is a village blacksmith, correct?"

"No," said Vanessa mildly, "actually he is a kindly old Duke."

"Exactly!" cried Rose. "Just as I thought!"

Rose Leigh had many other predictions, which she tried out on Vanessa at every opportunity, with an utter lack of accuracy they all agreed was uncanny. After a time the three women—Gypsy fortune-teller, moronic handmaiden, and romantic heroine—had developed a pleasant camaraderie. And in such cramped quarters, Vanessa no longer felt modest about undressing in front of her new friend.

She was doing just that on the last night of the voyage when Rose Leigh glanced over and noticed the small heart-shaped rash on her left thigh. Embarrased, Vanessa explained that it was a birthmark and not contagious.

"Now that is indeed odd," said Gypsy Rose Leigh

thoughtfully. "Only once in my life have I seen a birthmark such as that one."

"Really?" said Vanessa, mildly curious.

"Yes," said Rose, gesturing with a boa feather. "It was on the backside of an English monk in Sussex, about eighteen years ago. His name was Brother Al. He had come to me because I was supposed to be able to remove all manner of birthmarks with my Gyspy spells or, failing that, sandpaper."

"Were you able to remove it?"

"Nay," said Rose, dancing before a looking glass while she waved the feather boa back and forth. "It was an indelible mark on the poor monk's posterior. I say 'poor monk' because the man was incredibly pious. Almost as if he were doing penance for an enormous sin." She peered again at Vanessa's lush thigh. "Yes, they are identical."

"My thighs?" Vanessa asked brightly. "I should *hope* so."

"No, you ninny," Rose reproved, "the two birthmarks. And obviously I can no more remove your birthmark than his. 'Tis a shame, too, as you have an almost flawless body."

"I know, I *know*," said Vanessa, a trifle irritated. Everyone *talked* about her nearly flawless Beauty, but did anyone do anything about it?

On that note—an F sharp, it seemed to Vanessa's musically trained ear—they decided to go to sleep. On the morrow they would dock at New Orleans Harbor. It was going to be her first encounter with the New World, and Vanessa was determined to make the best of it. She couldn't help wondering, however, as she drifted off to sleep, whether there would be sufficient potential for romance in America to live up to her standards. Even if her One True Love was dead, or worse, inaccessible to her, she couldn't help feeling the old stirring of suppressed rapture within her. What lay ahead?

New Orleans was a mad bustle of noise, activity, and fish smells. Vanessa and Brigitte embraced their friend Rose Leigh as she went off to both seek and tell her fortune in the New World. Moments later, Vanessa spotted a tall Moor standing amidst the crowd, holding up a placard on which was written LADY VANESSA SHERWIN-WILLIAMS, and beneath that, in smaller letters, *New Orleans Coach and Limo, Limited*. Within moments, the two weary travelers were in an open coach as the Moor (here in America they called them Negroes, Vanessa remembered) guided them through the city's lively boulevards.

It certainly wasn't like the quiet streets of Devonshire. On every corner vendors hawked their Creole wares and groups of Negro musicians played hot, improvisational minuets to a rhythm she had never heard before—loud, syncopated, wailing. No future in that sort of distasteful music, she knew instinctively. Wrought-iron balconies graced every house and gentlemen with tall hats and fitted waistcoats walked the teeming streets amidst harlots and Cajuns of every description. The breeze from the bayou was fresh and strong, wafting with it the fragrance of shellfish, garlic, and sewage.

But then they came to a sight that disturbed her greatly. She tapped the driver on the back with a parasol.

"What, pray tell, is that?" she inquired.

"Dat's a slave auction, missy," the driver said politely. "Dey jes' come ober from Africa to be sold to all da massas an' other honkies hereabouts."

Vanessa was deeply shocked. There, on the auction block stood a strong, proud African with a sign around his neck, saying "8.8% Financing Available." She had heard about the inhumane practice, of course, but was unprepared for the sight. How barbaric! Vanessa thought, comparing it to English law, in which every man was equal as long as he was wellborn, male, and incredibly wealthy.

Vanessa wasn't sure she was going to like this rough

country and its rude people. It was certainly clear that this was not a proper place for romance. Still, she would serve out her sentence with Auntie Bellum and Uncle Ravenel with grace and forbearance, not to mention Brigitte.

As dusk fell, they were in the countryside outside New Orleans' city limits, and the coach headed down a dirt road hung with green vines and branches of weeping willows (Vanessa noticed a baby tree that was merely sniffling), and the aroma of magnolia blossoms invaded her perfect, rounded nostrils. Suddenly the trees gave way to a huge clearing in which stood a magnificent white plantation house. Vanessa realized she was at the home of her Auntie Bellum and Uncle Ravenel—*her* home for the next two years.

♡   ♡   ♡

"Ah hope y'all had a raht pleasant trip?" her Auntie Bellum warbled as Vanessa and Brigitte were led inside the stately home. Auntie Bellum was a stout woman in her late forties; she had a kind heart.

"No storms at sea, Ah trust?" bellowed Uncle Ravenel. He was short and stocky, but his most noticeable feature was a somewhat bulbous nose from which sprouted a thick crop of hairs. He was but a distant cousin of her father, the kindly old Duke, but she and her sisters were urged to call him and his wife "aunt" and "uncle." Occasionally one of the sisters would refer to them as "our poor white gar*bage* relatives from America."

"Except for the unease which visited my Person, it was pleasant enough," said Vanessa. She noticed her uncle and aunt cast uncomprehending glances at each other. Was it her accent? She would try again: "I threw up a lot," she ex-

plained. At this, her relatives beamed. The two cultures had
been bridged so quickly!

"Well, Ah 'spect you'll wanna get freshened up for
dinner," Auntie Bellum said, ushering Vanessa to her bedchamber and Brigitte to her alcove next door. "We have a
special surprise for y'all tonight."

At this, Uncle Ravenel chortled extremely loudly.

"What kind of surprise?" Vanessa asked her aunt as they
moved up the stairs.

"A . . . gen'man caller!" Auntie Bellum giggled. Another
chortle from downstairs, where Uncle Ravenal was evidently
listening.

For a moment, Vanessa's heart sped up, thinking invol-
untarily of her One True Love, but then it shifted into idle as
she realized her realtives were probably just indulging in a
little hopeful matchmaking. She was something of a catch,
she realized, for these poor relations.

Sure enough, an hour later, when she came down in the
taffeta gown her father had allowed her to purchase before
leaving England, there was her "gen'man caller": a tall, dark,
and torpidly handsome man with enormous waxed moustaches, which he twirled constantly.

"Beauregard, come meet our beautiful kin from England," said Uncle Ravenel, chortling so gleefully his nostril
hair unfurled like one of those New Year's noisemakers
Vanessa had seen. "Mah dear Vanessa, this is the proud and
unmarried son of one of New Orleans' oldest families—Mr.
Beau Weevil."

Vanessa, as always unfailingly polite, made the first
attempt at social conversation.

"My, Mr. Weevil. One of New Orleans' oldest families!
Just how old is that?"

Beau, who had taken off his dashing hat and was about to

sweep low with a bow, was apparently stumped by the question.

"Well . . . Ah don't rahtly know, Miz Vanessa. Mah daddy's in his early fifties, mah muthuh won't say, but Ah'd wager that don't make 'em the oldest folks in N'Awleans!"

So it was going to be one of *those* evenings.

Dinner was an ordeal for Vanessa. Uncle Ravenel and Auntie Bellum had obviously decided to impress some of their New Orleans friends by showing off their titled "niece" from England, and some of the guests did not fit Vanessa's definition of suitable dinner companions. Although the dinner was interesting—local delicacies including crawfish and toad pie—she was alarmed by the woman who ate her fish whole, bones and all, and distressed by the gentleman to her right who inquired incredulously if it were true that in England people bathed. After dessert—gumbo soufflé—the two young people, Beau and Vanessa, were left conspicuously alone in the parlor while the men went to one sitting room to gossip and the women remained to savor their cigars and brandy. Heavens, thought Vanessa, this was an odd country.

Her attention was soon diverted to a new situation: It appeared that Beau, who had been almost embarrassingly attentive to her over dinner, had clearly been smitten by her. From his demeanor here in the parlor, he was going to attempt to romance her, and as a professional, Vanessa could not help but be interested. She could hear shuffling behind the parlor door and assumed it was her aunt and uncle positioning themselves to hear. What would Beau's approach be like, and how would it differ from British romance? Would he be tempestuous or passionate? Reckless or gentle? Despite the fact that she felt no attraction for Beau himself, she looked forward to finding the answers to her sincerely felt questions. It was her destiny, she knew, to keep alert for the little tremors of love. One never knew.

BOOK III

Fate Spins on Its Heels

♡   ♡   ♡

If romance be the soup of love
Then how much more tragic the stew!
                            —*John Dunphy, 1794*

Chapter

7

♡　　　♡　　　♡

*B*eau Weevil sat on a tuffet, twirling his moustaches, thinking of what to say.

He rummaged through his cluttered mind and finally came up with something he felt appropriate to the circumstances:

"Tell me, Miz Vanessa," he said, his drawl as thick as gumbo pudding, "what's a nice gal lahk y'all doin' in a place lahk this?"

Beau sat back on the tuffet, satisfied. It was the sort of line that devastated local belles at singles balls.

But Vanessa was bitterly disappointed. It was a line that was already a cliché in its own time, a line lacking in the sort of finesse she hoped for in even the most minor of romantic encounters. She sighed inwardly.

"It should be perfectly clear what I am doing," she said, suppressing a trace of irritation. "I am partaking of an after-repast drink whilst I converse with you."

Beau cleared his throat and unabashedly tried again.

"Mebbe y'all'd like ta come back to mah place and see mah itchings?"

"That's *'etchings,'* " Vanessa corrected politely but firmly. "And, no, I should not like to."

Beau furrowed his brow in confusion. These overtures had been hugely successful with belles from all over the South. But with this young lady he seemed to be getting nowhere. Perhaps courting English aristocracy required a different approach from the one he was familiar with. As the quintessential southern gentleman, Beau was highly trained in three principal areas— romancing southern belles, gambling on riverboats, and whuppin' uppity slaves. But all this polite fussin' and froufrou was alien to his talents. Still, he had to admit this Vanessa gal was a heap more good-lookin' than most of the southern gals he had met during one-soiree stands. And her daddy, he knew, was a rich 'un. It was certainly worth continuing the effort and using some of that charm Beau was famous for throughout the parish of New Orleans.

"What's your sign?" he asked brightly, knowing this was irresistible to females of all nationalities.

Vanessa was no exception. "Lions rampant on a striped coat of arms, with a griffin below," she said promptly. She was proud that the Sherwin-Williamses could trace their ancestry several centuries back to King Richard the Lion-Hearted, though admittedly it was through Richard's in-laws.

Beau did not comprehand the response, though he was mildly encouraged that the conversation was still alive.

"How about a little nightcap?" he asked seductively.

"It's kind of you to offer," Vanessa said, "but I never sleep with any sort of garment upon my head."

"Uh-huh," said Beau disconsolately, giving up.

Just as an awkward silence threatened to descend upon the two of them, the parlor door swung open. Uncle Ravenel toppled headlong into the room, his hand still cupped to his ear, as Auntie Bellum rushed past him toward the couple. She was grinning from ear to nose, as her smile tended to be lopsided.

"Ah hope we haven't interrupted any billin', cooin', spoonin', or courtin'," Auntie Bellum said, giggling madly.

"No," Vanessa assured her, "none of the above. In fact, Mr. Weevil was just leaving. I feel I must retire to bed for my Beauty sleep. I am still suffering from a touch of sail-lag, as I am sure you will understand."

Perceiving this as a hint that he should depart, Beau rose and bowed sweepingly, raising a cloud of dust from the floor as he did so. Thereupon, he kissed the lovely hands of Vanessa, Auntie Bellum, and a bewildered Uncle Ravenel.

"Ah'm shore we'll be seein' more of each other," he said to Vanessa, who was doing her utmost to stifle a yawn. "Therefore, Ah won't say adieu."

They waited.

"Ah shall say au revoir, or, until we meet again."

They waited again.

"Which will it be?" asked Auntie Bellum a trifle impatiently.

"Until we meet again," Beau said finally, opting for the second choice. And in a flurry of bowing and a cloud of dust, he was off.

♡   ♡   ♡

As the days passed, it became clear that Beau was smitten with Vanessa, as he began sending her huge bouquets of cattails and Louisiana swamp grass. Each day, the postman always rang twice to deliver Beau's ardent missives, which contained such poetic sentiments as, "My soul is so bursting with love for you,

I've had to increase my shirt size," and "One day, I hope our hearts will beat as one, our eyes will blink as two, our toes will curl as ten . . ."

Whatever Beau lacked in eloquence, he more than made up for in ardor and sincerity, that much Vanessa had to admit. Yet she could not have felt the slightest stirrings of love toward him even had she tried. The reason was clear: She had promised her heart to another, far, far away, and she could not split her heart between two lovers. The thought of it was rather gruesome, in fact.

Thus, she politely declined most of Beau's entreaties for meetings, and whenever she did agree to rendezvous, she gently parried his obvious overtures so as not to hurt his feelings.

From time to time she would take a carriage into New Orleans and walk about moodily for hours in the French Quarter. The sights and sounds of the city would help her take her mind off her romantic despair. Occasionally, she would even mingle with the common people, taking rides on those horse-drawn streetcars with the quaint little names that New Orleans was famous for. Though she often rode the streetcar named Desire, she would have preferred one with a name more along her line—Rapture, perhaps.

Yet what Vanessa thought most about was being back home in Devonshire, in the arms of her One True Love.

Then one dreary afternoon it happened, an event that would alter her future. She had just returned from one of her strolls through the French Quarter and upon arriving back at the plantation, she noted she was the only one at home— except for the slave cook and pastry chef, Jemima. As she passed by the table in the front hallway, she happened to glance down and notice an envelope lying there unopened. It was addressed to her uncle Ravenel, and something looked familiar about the scrawl, though she could not think why.

Suddenly, she realized what had caught her eye: Of course! The handwriting was her father's! Though she stood there for a moment, feeling quite guilty, she knew at once she would *have* to open the envelope. First, it was the only practical way to read the letter inside; and second, she *had* to know what her father planned for her. If she did not open it, she would never find out her fate, for her uncle was too intimidated by her father's wealth and station to dare confide in her.

With trembling hands, she snatched up the letter and crept into the kitchen, where she kindly waved Jemima out the back door. Holding it over a teakettle, she steamed the envelope open and began to read her father's message.

When she got to the second page, she let out the most godforsaken scream of her young life.

The letter shook in her hands. If ever a moment called for a full-tilt, no-holds-barred swoon, this was it. And yet the news she had just read was so devastating, so horrible, so awesomely dreadful, she felt she could *not* allow herself to give into the rapturous imbalance that now threatened to overcome her. Courageously but numbly, she read and reread the terrible passages:

. . . I leave it to you, my ill-bred American cousin, to break the news gently to Vanessa, for you will recall that I am still capable of changing my Will and Last Testament in which you and Cousin Bellum are remembered. What you must do is to find a way of alleviating the shock when Vanessa hears that the young Duke of Earl is dead. As you know, Vanessa is taken to bouts of rapture and swooning at the slightest provocation.

Here are the details: The duel between the young Duke of Earl and Lord Gastleigh did indeed take place at the appointed time. The swordplay was fierce, and after several thrusts, some parries, and a few comos, Gastleigh was pierced smack in the brain by the Duke's sword, though thanks be to God, it missed any vital organ. The épée, however, remains impaled in Gastleigh's forehead, where it still lodges as I pen this missive.

This dreadful state of affairs may have had its effect on the young Duke and cad—though some say that a deeper sadness than the outcome of the duel was also affecting him. In any case, he was seen shortly thereafter, walking disconsolately along the Cliffs of Rover. A peasant woman saw him slip—or perhaps jump—and crash onto the deadly rocks below. We are still seeking his hopefully broken body.

I leave it to you, my provincial cousin, to inform Lady Vanessa of these matters and also of my decision that she is now free to return here to wed Lord Gastleigh. The union of our two noble houses should not be impeded by the fact of Gastleigh's having a sword permanently affixed to his fore-head, even though the poor chap often mistakes the dangling épée for a pendulum and thus often believes himself to be a grandfather clock. The delusions are transitory, and Vanessa should not be put off by the other handicaps Gastleigh's new state presents, such as the difficulty he has in turning abruptly in narrow doorways.

As always, I remind you, my untitled cousin, that by the terms of my Will and Last Testament. . .

Here Vanessa stopped reading for tears blurred her otherwise crystal-clear eyes. She still could not believe the news. The Duke of Earl . . . her beloved Anthony, brother or no brother . . . her One True Love . . . Dead!

This was the big one. This was truly it. Gone, vanished, forever amber was her One True Love! Her life was over. It was finished. Nothing mattered anymore.

Why? Why had it happened? Had he tripped over those treacherous Cliffs of Rover? Or . . . had he jumped? Had he jumped because of despair over their love? Was that it? What else could it be? It certainly could *not* have been a clumsy accident! Why, she knew that Anthony wore thick rubber soles on his walking boots. No, he had obviously gone over on purpose, mourning the fact that he could never possess her! How terrible! How tragic! How sensitive!

Clutching the letter in her slender hand, she walked mournfully back into the hallway, tossing the empty envelope on the table. Such was her grief that she cared not that it would be obvious she had opened another's mail, a severe nay-nay in civilized society of the time. But what did it matter if she were found out? Her life was over anyway. Dejectedly, she stumbled up the stairs to her chamber, fell upon her bed, and let the wellsprings that held back the floodwaters of the tidal wave of tears deluge forth with abandon.

♡　　　♡　　　♡

In the week that followed, Vanessa spent her days in a daze, speaking in a monotone, sulking in corners, moping in closets, and refusing Brigitte's earnest entreaties to take nourishment, be it baked, mashed, or French fried. She often stood stoically at her window, gazing out to sea, remembering that this was one thing romantic heroines always did in this sort of situation. Such was her grief that she even wore black, which was far from her best color.

In time, she finally consented to see Beauregard in the privacy of the parlor, not because she felt any comfort from his persistent though hackneyed articulations of love, but because his idle chatter allowed her to think, to take stock of her life. So the long afternoons would pass, Beau speaking endlessly of his love for Vanessa, while she stared moodily out the window. By this time Beau had ceased coming up with lines from singles balls and had replaced them with pleas to marry him.

"We could make beautiful music together, Vanessa," he would say.

"I doubt it," she would retort absently. "I never learned to play the ukulele."

And so it would go. It was on one of those afternoons that Vanessa, in considering the options open to her, came to realize how limited her Life Choices were: Either she returned to her beloved England to marry Lord Gastleigh—perish the thought!—or she could resign herself to a fate much closer at hand. . . .

She looked appraisingly at the babbling Beau Weevil. Surely he was handsome in his own way, especially if one overlooked his moustaches, the ends of which were about fifteen inches long when twirled and waxed. Though his taste in attire was not her preference—he often wore shirts with the laundry cardboard still inside—she could certainly alter that.

Did it really matter? Vanessa wondered. Now that her One True Love was deceased, she might as well marry a mongoose as a Gastleigh or a Weevil. Was betrothal to an English dolt preferable to betrothal to a Louisiana bounder? Didn't it amount to the same fate? At least Beau would not have a sword protruding from his forehead and thus would be less of an embarrassment to walk the streets or attend balls with. Yes, there were definite advantages. And in her present state of indifference, betrothal to Beau would be painless. Yes, she *could* do it. She could . . . marry him . . . and live out her life with numb serenity, clasping to her ripe yet modest bosom the secret of her undying love for the departed soul of another.

"It takes two to minuet," Beau was saying, clutching now at straws as he continued his hitherto unrequited campaign.

To Beau's immense surprise, this time Vanessa responded with a smile, albeit forced.

"Yes," she said. "It does take two to minuet."

Beau was staggered by her concurrence, and words escaped him. When the words returned, he stammered: "Does—does—does this mean . . . that you will . . . marry me?"

Vanessa paused. She knew that this would be a moment that would forever shape her destiny. Yet she was struck by the irony that this day—the day she had dreamt of all her life—meant so little to her. Without Anthony, what could it mean? And so she nodded, unable to bring herself to give her assent by means of voice and tongue.

Beau let out a whoop of joy, which was followed instantly by the door crashing open as Uncle Ravenel once again toppled into the room, hand cupped to ear, while his wife trampled over him in her haste to get to the couple. Auntie Bellum squealed as she trundled across the room.

"We couldn't help overhearing!" she shrieked. "We'all are so happy for y'all both!" She threw a massive arm around Vanessa's slender shoulders. "Why, we'll throw the grandest party anyone evah saw in these heah pahts!"

Vanessa held up a pale hand. "I am sorry, Auntie," she said. "Beau and I would rather elope. Right, Beau?"

Auntie Bellum pouted. Uncle Ravenel, too, looked crestfallen, but quickly retrieved his crest and looked expectantly at Beau. Her groom-to-be was about to protest, but thought better of it as Vanessa fanned her eyelashes at him.

"That's raht," he said. "We just cain't wait for no weddin'. Why, Ah know a French preacher who'll marry us raht quick. Befo' you know it, we can be aboard a steamboat headin' upriver to a honeymoon in the Poconos." He paused uncertainly. "You *do* want a honeymoon, dontcha, Miz Vanessa?"

Vanessa nodded, shuddering inwardly. Men! Is that all they thought about?

"Well, then, it's all set. We'll do it this very afternoon!" exclaimed Beau.

"How wonderful," exclaimed Auntie Bellum, feeling mollified. "This calls for a drink! Ravenel, why don't you bring out the best we have—perhaps that lovely Arkansas champagne?"

♡   ♡   ♡

Later that evening they were in front of a crusty old preacher in the French Quarter, she holding a bouquet of the finest Delta ragweeds, he sporting a top hat and gloves. In attendance were Uncle Ravenel and Auntie Bellum as witnesses for Beau and, of course, Brigitte as both maid of honor and official French interpreter.

The preacher was a forgetful old pastor who spoke not a word of the King's tongue. His French was evidently a little odd, Vanessa noticed, because to judge by Brigitte's translations, his religious remarks did not always seem relevant to the point at hand. Toward the end of the ceremony came the critical words:

"Maintenant je vous prononce homme et femme," said the old minister.

Brigitte translated swiftly:

"Mandy, I pronounce homage to your farm."

Vanessa more or less had the drift, but felt a little something had been lost there. The old clergyman closed the prayer book and smiled toothlessly at Beau.

"Vous pouvez embrasser votre epouse, monsieur."

The simultaneous translation from Brigitte:

"You must go pooh to your embarrassed spouse, mister."

Beau was confused by the preacher's instructions, but Vanessa quickly guessed at the nuances in her lady-in-waiting's translation and indicated that Beau should kiss the bride. He did so, with southern gusto. Vanessa could hardly feel it, as she was anesthetized by her secret grief.

Minutes later they were outside the chapel, being pelted by cotton balls (rice was not a cash crop in the South) and on their way by carriage. They were headed for their reserved suite aboard the *Princess Dixie,* one of the finest steamboats on the mighty Mississippi. Uncle Ravenel had tied old boots and a stray cat to the back of their carriage, so there was plenty of noise as they drove through the cobblestone streets of New Orleans to the cheers of bystanders. Arriving at the Mississippi dock, they prepared to embark.

Her uncle and aunt had brought Brigitte with them in their carriage, as she would accompany her mistress aboard the steamboat, though she would sleep in a steerage cubbyhole to give the lovers their privacy. Now Auntie Bellum took Vanessa's face in her hands, bussed her repeatedly, and then said to Beau, "You be gentle with her, hear?" Uncle Ravenel shook Beau's hand hard and said to Vanessa, "Don't forget to tell your pappy, bless his wealthy soul, that I paid for the bouquet."

Then they were up on deck, waving down, as the huge paddle wheel began its rotation. She almost felt a surge of excitement at the adventure she was embarking upon, but immediately felt guilty. To think that at this very moment her Lover's body was probably being swept ashore somewhere, possibly some rock-strewn beach in Spain or Switzerland! Oh, God! What right did she have to feel excitement over life when her One True Love had quite possibly given his life for their love?

As Beau took her elbow to lead her to their stateroom, she realized she had another problem to contend with this evening. Soon, she knew, after they'd feasted at supper, he would return to their cabin and want to have . . . his . . . way with her. All men were the same that way, she knew, and it was the price she always sensed she would have to pay for romance. Though what romance had to do with "it," she could not imagine. It was such a shame, really, that love had to turn so . . . icky. She nevertheless decided to bear it stoically, as she did all things. For she knew, as she walked down the imposing hallways of this steamboat, paddling its way to the headwaters of the mighty Mississippi, where the swirling waters met the majestic Poconos, that this was more than a honeymoon—it was her destiny calling yet again, although this time with an infinitely sadder cry.

Chapter

8

♡   ♡   ♡

he *Princess Dixie*—known familiarly to travelers up and
down the river as the *Princess Di*—was a cornucopia of
humanity come together on the mighty Mississippi's most famous paddle boat. Fur trappers, gamblers, pioneers, merchants,
and slave retailers crowded its long sleek decks by day and its
velvet-tufted dining rooms by night. The air of gaiety everywhere was contagious. Even heartsick Vanessa was lifted out of
her doldrums that first night as she sat at the Captain's table with
her new husband, looking around with keen interest at the
assortment of characters about her. So this was what they called
the Great Chamber Pot of America!

To her left, she noticed a group of hardy settlers entering
the dining room. The headwaiter guided the scruffy band to a
table, shouting, "Donner, Party of twelve!" No sooner had the
pioneers been seated than they began tearing the flesh off their
T-bone steak entrées. Somewhat shocked by their manners,
Vanessa was informed by the Captain that these settlers would

be traveling west through the Rockies by Conestoga wagons, and this riverboat would be their last chance for a decent repast. The Captain, a literate fellow named Twain, was helpful to Vanessa, though quite hopeless as a storyteller.

Sitting alone at a table to her right was a gentleman dressed in a fine waistcoat. Though not unattractive, he had jug ears and badly spaced teeth, a thin moustache, and dark hair that fell partly across his forehead in a rakish comma. She could see on the table before him a riverboat ticket punched for "Tara, Georgia." What Vanessa found most odd about this man was his intense concentration as he muttered to himself. He appeared to be rehearsing something he intended to say. First he said, "Candidly, my dear, I don't give a hoot!" Then he shook his head and tried again: "Confidentially, my dear, I couldn't care less!" Evidently still unsatisfied, he tried another version: "In all frankness, my dear, you can go take a flying leap. . . ." Vanessa averted her ears, a difficult anatomical feat at the best of times.

But it was at her own table that Vanessa was about to get a true earful. A horrid personage, loud and uncouth, had been seated at the Captain's table for reasons other than his breeding, which Vanessa estimated at subzero. He was unshaven and wore matted, putrid furs from head to toe. The fact that the furs were mostly mink added somewhat to his tolerability, but not much. The Captain explained apologetically that he was a French fur trapper who gave the riverboat much of his business by buying expensive dinners and gambling away his money. Vanessa could see that the Frenchman was already quite drunk, and was yelling and pounding the table in glee over a joke he had just told about having a fly in his soup.

"*Garçon!*" he demanded loudly of the waiter. "Do you have zee frogs' legs, *peut-être?*"

"Yes, sir," the waiter responded.

"Zen hop into zee kitchen and get me some cheeken!"

At that, the trapper burst into loud, raucous laughter, pounding a small, swarthy bald man sitting next to him on the back. Captain Twain felt obliged to introduce the boisterous trapper to the other diners at the table, commencing with Vanessa, who could hardly refrain from flaring her nostrils at the fellow's stench.

"Mrs. Weevil, may I present Trapper Jacques—hunter extraordinaire of mink, mongoose, and badger."

The odorous trapper's laughter subsided as he beheld Vanessa's heart-stopping Beauty. He leaned across the table and kissed her flawless hand, staining it. *"Mon plaisir, mademoiselle,"* he said, speaking a language Vanessa had never heard.

"A hunter of badger!" she exclaimed, feigning polite interest. "How very interesting. I have never seen a badger. Could you show me one?"

The trapper laughed uproariously. "Badger?" he snarled. "I ain't got no badgers! I ain't gotta show you no stinkin' badgers!"

Bewildered by the reply, Vanessa coughed delicately and turned her attention to the brown-skinned, bald gentleman sitting at Trapper Jacques's side.

"And who, pray tell, is this man?" she asked politely.

"Heem? A feelthy savage," Trapper Jacques said, swatting the guant but fastidious fellow on the head with a spoon. The bald man seemed to enjoy being struck, for he smiled.

The Captain made the necessary introduction.

"He is Trapper Jacques's faithful Indian companion, Gandhi," he explained. "All trappers are required by law to have faithful Indian companions."

As Vanessa smiled at the man, he smiled back, pressed his fingers together, and said, "Tenk you veddy much." How exciting! Vanessa thought. A real Indian! Weren't they the ones who lived in wigwams? Or was that ashrams? No, they were the ones who smoked that strange tobacco in their pipes! Or was it tea? Or spices? No, that was China . . . Oh, dear. Geography always had been *such* a bother for her.

She would have enjoyed continuing the conversation with the strange savage had she not been interrupted by Beauregard, who was impatient to get on with the honeymoon's main event. Throughout dinner, he had repeatedly glanced at his pocket watch, nudged Vanessa in her perfectly formed ribs, and yawned expansively. When these hints had failed, he commenced to make lewd gestures with his napkin ring while waggling his eyebrows suggestively, gestures whose subtlety were lost on Vanessa. She, in the meantime, dawdled over her coffee and custard, asking for refills of both repeatedly.

"Lordy!" Beau said, stretching his arms, "it shore is mahty late. Ah'm 'bout ready to hit the old hay. How 'bout you, darlin'?"

Vanessa, unfamiliar with certain American idioms, asked, "Why would anyone care to assault hay, Beau?"

"Ah mean, darlin'—"

"He mins," Trapper Jacques said leeringly, "zat eet eez time for *les* newlyweds to make zee whoofkie-poofkie. Eef you ketch *mon* dreeft."

Vanessa ignored what she suspected were vulgar insinuations and continued dawdling with her ninth custard as the other diners retired for the night and the busboys began to clear the tables. Beau stared disconsolately at the cups stacked atop one another in front of Vanessa.

"Eef she was my weff," Jacques said gruffly, "I would teck her by zee hair and dregg her to zee cabine. Zat eez what a real man would do!"

Vanessa again ignored the loutish Frenchman. What was uppermost in her mind was to continue stalling Beau, and what she needed was a distraction. At that very moment, fortune intervened: She heard off to one side the sound of cards and the announcement that a high-stakes poker game was about to commence. Since the most awkward part of the upcoming ordeal was having to undress in the same room at the same time, she might be able to at least avoid that indignity by appealing to Beau's gambling instincts.

"Beau, my dear, why don't you join the game for half an hour?" she asked sweetly. "Then, when you return, I . . . shall be . . . waiting for you."

Would the ruse work? Vanessa wasn't sure, but she suspected Beau would be tempted. Her suspicion was grounded in the fact that as the sounds of the game increased, Beau had begun to shuffle the dinner plates absently.

"Well, all raht, darlin'," said Beau, putting up a poor show of reluctance as he knocked over his chair in his eagerness to get to the poker table. He gave her a peck on the cheek and dashed across the room. Vanessa could not help noticing, from the sudden freshness in the air around her, that Trapper Jacques had also departed for the poker game. She noticed the Frenchman sitting at the poker table, grinning lecherously at her through blackened teeth, drinking whiskey out of a brown jug, now and then giving his faithful Indian sidekick a kick in the side. What a cad! she thought. And what an odor! She wondered if the trapper bothered to skin the animals he killed or simply wore them.

Once back in her stateroom, she bolted the door shut and decided to prepare for the coming ordeal. Though she had received no formal education in lovemaking, she had read all a young lass needed to know about the subject. Shortly after puberty her governess had given her a copy of the best-selling manual, *The Grief of Sex*. It seemed simple enough to a British girl of her era: All she was supposed to do was shut her eyes as tightly as possible, keep her legs crossed as tightly as possible, and moan as if afflicted by stomach cramps. According to the manual, the entire messy business was not supposed to take more than ten seconds. Still, she was by no means happy about the coming assault upon her Person.

To relax, and perhaps better prepare herself for the inevitable, Vanessa took a long bath in the stateroom tub, anointing her near-flawless anatomy with oils and perfumes, letting the liquids run down the perfect contours of her smooth, velvety skin. . . . In short, she took her basic bath. (See Chapter Four for details.)

She then took out of her traveling chest a beautiful nightgown her Auntie Bellum had picked out for her—Brigitte, now asleep in the next room, called it a *niggle-jee*—and she held it to her bounteous body. Suddenly she noticed something: Why, the nightgown was full of holes! How shoddy! Holes everywhere! How could she keep her near-perfect body warm in such a drafty garment? Thank goodness she had remembered her sewing kit.

After threading a darning needle, she put on a warm robe, sat on the edge of the bed, and proceeded to correct the nightgown's faults. Time passed as the gentle rocking of the boat melded with the thrumming of the steam engine, causing her to doze off.

♡   ♡   ♡

She awakened some time later to a pounding at the door. Rubbing her eyes, she rose from the bed, tossed the *niggle-jee* aside, and went toward the door. The rapping continued insistently. That Beauregard! So eager! So impatient! So gross!

"Coming," she said irritably, though that was the last thing she felt like doing that evening. She walked hesitantly to the door and unlatched it.

The door swung open. There, in the light from the ship's

corridor, was Trapper Jacques, leaning unsteadily against Gandhi.

Vanessa clutched her robe to her perfect white neck.

"Wha—wha—what are *you* doing here?" she stammered.

"Bon soir, ma petite Vanessa," said Trapper Jacques. To his faithful Indian companion, struggling to support his weight on his bony shoulders, the Frenchman said, "She eez some piece of *boeuf,* eh, Gandhi?"

"Whatever you want, I'm sure it can wait until tomorrow," Vanessa said, attempting to shut the door. But Jacques blocked it with a foot clad entirely in otter fur.

"What I want weel not wait unteel tomorrow," Jacques said, pushing his way into her room.

"Monsewer!" said Vanessa fluently. "You will either leave my room at once or I shall call the stewards and have you ejected for unlawful entry!"

At that, Trapper Jacques guffawed.

"Unlawfool? Zat eez to leff!" exclaimed Jacques. "I em *parfaitement* weezeen my rights to be heere. Thees eez my cabin now and you are *my* woman!"

"Wha—wha—what do you mean?" asked Vanessa.

"I mean zat your 'usband, Beauregard, lost you to me at zee cards tonight!"

Vanessa was appalled!

Apparently she had been bet and lost by her husband of a few hours! How *could* Beau have been so rash! And to this . . . this . . . animal!

"Are you trying to say my husband lost me in a poker game?" she asked, backing away, playing for time.

"Slap Jack," said Jacques. Trained as she was in obedience, Vanessa reared back and slapped Jacques across his scraggly face.

"Eu!" shouted Jacques. "Why deed you slap me on zee cheek?"

"You said to," said Vanessa. "You said slap Jacques, did you not?"

"*Non*, I said Slap Jack."

Again Vanessa obeyed, her hand stinging from the trapper's beard and assorted parasites within.

Angered, Trapper Jacques came closer.

"I warn you, sir!" she protested. "Do not lay a hand upon my Person or I shall cry out!"

But Jacques continued his pursuit until he had cornered her, appropriately, in the corner. "You geev me beeg kees now, eh?"

"Never!" Vanessa shouted. "I would not kiss you if you were the last pair of lips in the universe!"

"What eez wrong? You do not like Jacques?" he asked, sensing a lack of popularity.

"Like you? Like you?" Vanessa laughed bitterly. "I think you are a horrible, filthy, loudmouthed, uncouth wretch of a man!"

Jacques perked up. "Zen zer eez some hope for us, yes?" he inquired.

Sighing, Vanessa realized that logic was hopeless. As the eager Frenchman moved closer, she searched frantically about the cabin for some means to escape. If she could get away, surely someone would protect her. Perhaps even Beauregard, the cad. Then she thought of a way: the porthole in the privy. All she had to do was convince Trapper Jacques she needed some privacy.

"Would you excuse me, sir?" she asked. This so surprised Trapper Jacques that he ceased his approach.

"Eu?" he said.

"I am unprepared for . . . whatever you may have in mind, sir," she said, playing it demure. "I must take my bath first."

"Bath?" Jacques asked. "What eez zees bath?"

It was Vanessa's turn to be surprised.

"You do not know?" she asked. "It involves something called soap and something called water."

"Zee water I know," Jacques said. "But zee soap I never heard from."

Vanessa held her ground. "I *must* have my bath," she said, folding her arms and tapping her feet.

It worked. Apparently dumbfounded by this odd British custom of bathing, Trapper Jacques shrugged and allowed her to enter the privy.

♡ ♡ ♡

There was no time to waste. Once inside the privy, Vanessa slipped into a dress and put her beautifully rounded head through the similarly shaped porthole and looked up. The promenade deck, thanks be to God, was but a few feet above the porthole. Why, she could climb through, reach for the railing above, and pull herself to the deck. The only real problem was whether she could slip out of the porthole without creasing her dress.

Somehow, she managed to wriggle through the window and hoist her bodacious form upward to the promenade. The only belonging she carried with her was a purse into which she had haphazardly thrown some bank notes, some rouge, some mascara, lipstick, eyeliner, a hairbrush, a tortoiseshell comb, an emery board, fourteen bottles of perfume, some scented talc, and a change of undies.

Dawn was breaking and the deck was beginning to fill with passengers walking briskly up and down the promenade, taking their morning constitutionals and declarationals. She tried to make herself as inconspicuous as possible. One passenger, a Japanese tourist weighed down by a huge daguerreotype camera dangling from his neck, bowed as he passed Vanessa. Suddenly she caught her breath: Over by a lifeboat was none other than Beauregard!

Striding toward him, she swung her purse in a huge arc and struck him fully upon the top of his head.

"Vanessa!" he cried, rubbing his head.

"Scoundrel!" she exclaimed.

"Aw, Vanessa, Ah know, Ah know!" he cried sheepishly. "It was the last hand of the evenin', and Ah was tahrd of slappin'. He slapped the last Jack and Ah lost everythin'!"

"How *could* you bet your own wife!" Vanessa cried.

"Ah'm real sorry 'bout that part of it, Vanessa," he said. "Ah never lost a wife afore in a card game." He looked thoughtful for a moment. "Ah *did* lose some sheep once, and a set of bone china. But never a wife." He scratched his cheek. " 'Course Ah never been married before," he said with a feeble chuckle.

Vanessa found her former husband's attempt at levity to be in poor taste. Her rancor was interrupted, however, by a familiar odor that came floating down the promenade. Looking through the morning mist, she recognized Trapper Jacques and his Indian sidekick, prowling the deck, evidently searching for her.

"Quick!" said Vanessa. "Hide me, Beau! Please!"

Beauregard, guilty over having lost a wife on the very night of his wedding, was ready to make up for it. As Trapper Jacques's steps grew closer, he lifted the tarpaulin of a nearby lifeboat and gestured for Vanessa to climb in. Hurriedly, Vanessa hied herself to her hiding place.

Seconds later, Jacques and Gandhi were at Beauregard's side and Vanessa could hear him ask about her whereabouts.

To Vanessa's great relief, Beau played dumb, a ruse that required very little acting on his part.

"Ah'll help y'all look for her," declared Beau loudly. "Mah honor demands it!" God bless the silly boy, thought Vanessa gratefully.

She remained crouched inside the lifeboat for what seemed like either an eternity or about fifteen minutes, Vanessa wasn't quite sure. From her hiding place she could hear the sounds of Trapper Jacques's footsteps followed by the sound of the back of his hand whacking Gandhi upon the head. Once, she even heard a disconsolate Brigitte call her name, but she dared not respond.

Presently, good fortune smiled upon her when the *Princess Di* made an unscheduled stop to recoal by the banks of the wide Missouri, which flowed into the mighty Mississippi not far from the wimpy Wabash. At the dock, as slaves shoveled coal into the bowels of the riverboat, Vanessa leapt from her hiding place and ran down the solitary gangplank. Looking around, she noticed a waterfront café and ran inside. Walking directly to the ladies' privy, she huddled inside a pay chamber-pot stall until the *Princess Di*'s whistle sounded and the huge riverboat paddled away up the mighty Mississippi.

It took Vanessa a moment to realize it, but she was . . . finally free! Free from exile, free from her marriage to Beau, free from reeking Trapper Jacques! True, she was a woman alone, in a strange land, with no friends and a minimum of makeup. But Vanessa was nothing if not resourceful. Somehow she would secure passage on a riverboat back to New Orleans! Somehow she would find a berth on the clipper bound for England!

Emerging from the café, she wandered down to the bustling docks where cargo was being toted and untoted. There, she saw a most unusual thing: Several people were standing on a bearded man who lay prone upon the ground. When she looked a little closer, she noted a distinct resemblance between this bearded gentleman and her Jewish tailor in Devonshire.

Her curiosity aroused, she asked a tall Negro standing nearby why these people were standing on the gentleman.

"Why, dey be standin' on de Levy," said the Negro. "Standin' on de Levy, waitin' for de *Robert E Lee.*"

"Oh," said Vanessa, not understanding but too fatigued to ask for further explanation. "And where does the *Robert E. Lee* go?"

"Why, he be gwine down ta N'Awrleans, missy."

And so Vanessa joined the others standing on the Levy, awaiting not only the *Robert E. Lee* —but her destiny.

Chapter

9

♡   ♡   ♡

*V*anessa's sea voyage homeward to her beloved England was beset by turbulent weather, keeping her cabinbound for the duration of the journey. It was almost as if Poseidon's heinous wrath raged in perfect cosmic union with the tempestuous storm of emotion that tore apart the very rafters of her tortured heart. Or something like that. Each thunderclap was like a dagger piercing her heart; each lightning bolt struck at the very core of her Being. Heaven itself, it seemed, was weeping copious tears of rain and blowing its celestial nose in her haggard, yet still flawlessly beautiful countenance.

Her forced seclusion within the confines of her stateroom afforded Vanessa ample opportunity to reflect seriously upon the abundance of tragedy that had befallen her. And what a swell tragedy it was, worthy of the most steadfast of romantic heroines! Vanessa could not suppress an immodest twinge of pride at what she had undergone in the name of love. Within the space of a few short months, she had found True Love, lost True

Love, temporarily misplaced True Love, slapped True Love, grieved the demise of True Love, been wed to False Love, been lost in a card game to Odorous Love! . . . All this and *still* a virgin!

Throughout her cabinbound reflections, one question kept repeating itself over and over in her mind: *Why me?*

But of course there was no answer to that question, for it had been asked many times before, throughout the millennia, by those more worthy of an answer than she—by philosophers, theologians, and Hebrew complainers from the Bible. And yet, she could not help but reflect on the arbitrary whims of Fate and the heartbreak and remorse it had caused her. This was the kind of person she was—romantic, yes, but deeply thoughtful nonetheless.

Vanessa set about buffing her nails.

In the midst of her contemplations and labor, a more pressing problem entered her beautifully furrowed brain. During the hard trek after fleeing Trapper Jacques and the nightmare of the riverboat, she had only one thing on her mind—to escape this barbaric New World and to return to the pleasant, if slightly irritating, life she knew in England. But now, as she lay upon her bunk, she commenced to wonder what she would do once she had arrived at her homeland.

To begin with, her One True Love was dead, so he was out of the picture, romancewise. True, Lord Gastleigh was still alive, but his handicap made him less likely as a candidate than ever. Would her father, the kindly old Duke, still insist on their betrothal? After all, her marriage to Beauregard Weevil was, in the eyes of the Church, annulled due to nonconsummation. Vanessa blushed deeply. And if Lord Gastleigh still wanted her, how would she feel attending balls accompanied by a husband with a dueling sword protruding from his forehead? How could they dance close? How would they dip? No, it was out of the question. She would marry no one. She would preserve herself forever for . . . for . . . for whom?

The answer to this question did not come immediately to her. But as she considered it at length, buffing her nails to a flawless gloss, it occurred to her that romantic heroines in her sort of dilemma generally had two options available to them: to join a convent or . . . to commit suicide, neither of them much of a bargain. Yes, it was becoming clear now: Vanessa would have to choose one or the other.

Then one night, as the thunder clapped and the lightning applauded, the answer came to her in a dream. As usual, she was in a deep reverie. There came an eager knock on the porthole, seemingly waking her from her slumber. Who could it be in the middle of the vast Atlantic, especially at this time of night? She opened her eyes to get a better look and, immediately, shock overcame her. Outside, flying beside the ship, was her One True Love, borne aloft in a pair of brand-new angel's wings! Oh, Love! Was it really he? She called out to him, but he spoke not, the effort of staying aloft in the updrafts taking all his concentration for the moment.

Then suddenly and miraculously, the ghostly figure floated through the porthole and stood before her! It was her Dream Lover, all right, sopping wet, his wings drooping with salt water. How radiant he looked! How pale! How badly in need of a shave!

"Come," he said in a ghostly yet virile voice. "Come to me. We can reunite in Heaven above. You will be happy there, my love. Everything is so much calmer . . . so much happier . . . so much cheaper . . . I beseech you, Vanessa, come to me!"

"How? How? How?" cried out Vanessa, not catching on.

The angel, alias her One True Love, rolled his eyes. He would have to give her a hint. He brought his hand up to his throat and made a cutting gesture. He then held an imaginary noose above his head and let his tongue loll out of his mouth.

At that, Vanessa suddenly understood what she was being beckoned to do and she ran to him, her arms outstretched. But alas, he was only thin air (though deeply bronzed and muscled) and she ran through his image and rammed headfirst into the stateroom wall. As she shook her precious head, the angel vanished as quickly as he had appeared. And in that moment, she awoke with a start to find herself alone in the cabin.

Now she knew what she must do! Without a moment to waste, she slipped out of her bedclothes, threw on her dress, brushed her hair 560 times, put on her eyeliner, etc., and left the cabin with a determination she had not felt in all her young years.

On deck, the storm was raging with a fury unparalleled in the annals of sea lore. The ship lumbered through the wash, masts creaking, decks rolling with seawater. Holding on to the guide ropes, Vanessa made her way across the deck, hiding behind the mizzenmast so as not to be seen by the ship's crew—especially as the tempest had badly mussed her raven-black flaxen hair. Moments later, when the coast was clear, she climbed atop the ship's railing. Below her, the sea raged. Waves the size of houses, though not furnished, slammed against the ship's hull. She held on to a thick rope as she brought her perfectly formed legs over the side. She was moments away from her final glimpse of life. Slowly, slowly, she loosened her grip, sliding downward into the churning waters. Any instant now, she would be gone, reunited forever with her One True Love . . . Going, going . . .

" 'Ey there!" came a booming voice, cutting across the storm's din.

Mortally embarassed to be glimpsed thus, ankles bared to the elements, Vanessa held on to the rope.

"Cease and desist!" came the voice of an obviously

grizzled bosun's mate. "Passengers are not allowed to disembark until the ship has come to a complete stop! This is for your own safety and convenience!"

"Oh," said Vanessa, swinging her legs modestly back onto the deck. She was mortified. "Dreadfully sorry."

As the sailor helped her down from her suicidal aerie, it all became blindingly clear to her. Of course! It was Fate again! In the person of a lowly bosun's mate, Fate had intervened to save her life! God, in His infinite wisdom, had chosen this rough sailor as His messenger! Perhaps He was saving her for some greater glory! Perhaps there was to be some meaning to her life! Perhaps her own intentions had been transformed into some overriding purpose!

Perhaps she was overintellectualizing the whole thing.

Back in her cabin, her suicide attempt foiled, Vanessa contemplated her alternative future. With suicide no longer one of the options open to her, and with these heavy religious overtones all over the place, she suddenly knew what she should do once the ship reached England: Get off.

"After that," she averred to herself, "we'll see."

♡   ♡   ♡

Several days later, in clear weather, Vanessa was thrilled to see the Cliffs of Rover once again. Penniless, haggard, and heartsick, Vanessa disembarked in Southampton and was immediately caught up in the bustle of activity at the wharf. After going rapidly through customs, where she was asked if she had anything to declare and replied, naturally, "My undying love," she looked about in momentary confusion.

In the last several days, she had come to realize what she must do. It was fitting, it was right, it was appropriate. But how *did* one join a convent? Which convent was right for her?

Were there applications? Credit references? Where should she start her search for spiritual peace and serenity?

All these questions and more were suddenly answered in a mysterious way, as if that celestial spirit of yore were up to its old tricks again. There, right at wharfside next to a fast-repast tavern named Fish McChips, was a small booth. Inside was a sister of the cloth, recruiting for a nearby nunnery. The docks were particularly fertile territory for the good sister, since there were daily shiploads of fallen romantic heroines returning from the New World with only one choice left to them. At desks spread out across the docks, girls much like Vanessa (though not as flawless in their Beauty) were filling out applications, while the sister called out, "Join a Convent, Flee the World."

Within moments Vanessa had an application in her slim and beauteous hand and began to answer the questions, many of which were multiple-choice:

OUR LADY OF THE MOPING MARTYRS

An Equal Opportunity Nunnery—Sussex, England

1. Have you ever communicated with God?
2. What did He say?
3. How was His Grammar?
4. Do you believe in Papal Infallibility, the Feast of the Assumption, or the Tooth Fairy? (Check one)
5. Do you vow to emulate Saint Ignatia, who suffered terrible torture and martyrdom rather than renounce her Church or her virtue?

STOP: DO NOT TURN PAGE UNTIL
YOU ARE TOLD TO DO SO

To Be Answered Only by Fallen Romantic Heroines

1. Have you recently found and lost True Love?
2. Did you find that your True Love was related to you in any way?
3. Did your father ship you off to an exile far, far away from your One True Love?
4. To New Orleans, Australia, or Detroit?
5. Did you get married to someone you didn't love?
6. Did you . . . you know?
7. How did you attempt suicide, which is a sin?
8. Was it bloody, as it was for the Blessed Martyrs?
10. When parallel parking a carriage, is it best to put the horse into reverse before beginning to turn?

After completing her application, Vanessa handed it to the head nun at the booth, Sister Carrie. It was marked on the spot, and Vanessa was told that she had a flawless score. Awaiting the scores of scores and scores of other recruits, Vanessa stood by the booth and decided that she would become truly religious. This was her true vocation, she decided. She would love God as she had loved her One True Love. This is what she had been waiting to find: reckless tranquillity.

As soon as the other recruits had been gathered together, Sister Carrie herded them toward several waiting carriages, emblazoned with the convent's colors—black and light black.

In moments they were off, rolling down a pleasant road, while Sister Carrie led them in several religious hymns such as "Abide with Me" and "Thank Heaven for Little Girls."

In the gently swaying carriage, filled to the brim with would-be nuns, Vanessa found herself squeezed next to a pretty, red-haired girl with freckles and a wide, tooth-filled smile. Her blue eyes shone like the finest rubies. Her name was Shannon O'Herlihy, she told Vanessa, and since she was already a Catholic, she would be happy to help Vanessa through her first days in the novitiate. They would both be equally new, of course, but Shannon at least knew what saints had been martyred in what fashion, and that was an advantage.

It turned out that Shannon was also a fallen romantic heroine. She had found True Love, lost True Love, given True Love a blow on the shins, grieved the loss of True Love, been sold into white slavery by a wicked uncle, and escaped, only to be married to a cad who lost her during a game of whist to a mysterious Bulgarian.

When Vanessa explained that she, too, had suffered many of these same romantic tragedies, Shannon exclaimed, "We have so much in common! Isn't it surprising that there should be so many coincidences in Life!"

At this, Vanessa was hard-pressed to hide her smile. Poor innocent Shannon, she thought. She was obviously less well-versed in romance than Vanessa was, else she would have known that coincidences are the stuff of love.

"Coincidences are the stuff of love," Vanessa explained patiently.

"Why, I was just thinking the exact same thing!" Shannon cried.

The carriage was rattling down a lonely stretch of road, bordered on both sides by deep woods. Suddenly Sister

Carrie said to the girls in the carriage, "Draw the curtain, girls. There are Highwaymen along this road!" The girls all gasped. "We can't afford to risk virtue this close to nunhood!" exclaimed the good sister. The girls all complied, hunching down in their seats. Soon, however, they were past Highwayman territory and in a safer neighborhood.

As Vanessa and Shannon chatted, Vanessa told her more about herself, her family, and her adventures with Brigitte, the poor lady-in-waiting she was forced to leave behind on the mighty Mississippi. Shannon seemed to become more thoughtful. Then, after Vanessa had told her how Brigitte had prepared potato tea after one particular romantic mishap, Shannon declared:

"Why, that sounds like my poor cousin Bridget!" Shannon became excited, and her brogue became more pronounced. "Sure, and it must be her! Was her potato compote truly horrendous?"

"Horrendous would be putting it mildly," said Vanessa mildly.

"Then perhaps my Bridget is your Brigitte!" Shannon declared. "Yes, I recall that she ran away from Dublin when she was but a teenage colleen! We even got a postcard from her saying she had taken a job as a lady-in-waiting with a Duke's family!"

"Impossible," sniffed Vanessa. "My Brigitte is quite French, I'm afraid."

That settled the matter as far as Vanessa was concerned. Even in the area of coincidences, especially as it regarded the Irish, one had to draw the line somewhere, else coincidence enter the realm of absurdity.

♡   ♡   ♡

The convent was everything Vanessa thought it would be, and much less. Perched high on a many-splendored hillock, the nunnery stood like a chimerical fortress, a haven for ladies in romantic distress. An air of calm serenity pervaded the area and wildlife was ever present on the verdant grounds.

As the stretch-carriage approached the convent bearing its load of pious pulchritude, Vanessa felt a shiver of delicious anticipation course through her exquisite body.

So she was going to be a nun!

It was going to be so lonely and forlorn and tragic, who knew what deliciously austere developments might come to pass! But in the meantime she intended to be incredibly religious. Not for her merely a place to get far from the madding crowd. No half-measures for her! If she was going to get cloistered, she was going to get good and cloistered. It was her fate to do things passionately, and piety was no exception.

And why should it be? It all depended on how one looked at it, Vanessa mused. Why, there would be new gowns, though admittedly of the black, evening-wear variety, and that was always exciting. She understood there were also some jewelry beads passed out to new nuns, and she rather liked the sound of that. And apparently nuns spent vast amounts of time in meditation—why, that was just a step away from reveries, which were, needless to say, right up Vanessa's aisle.

"Here we are, girls," said Sister Carrie sweetly as the stretch-carriage pulled up in front of the massive gate shielding those within from the world without. "Now I shall confiscate thy purses and thy worldly belongings before entering. Thou shalt have no need for them henceforth. We shall donate all of it to the poor."

Vanessa gasped. Could her fate be going awry? Her

purse, confiscated? Where was the sense in that? Could the poor look half as attractive in eyeliner as she did? No, this would not do at all. She would have to suspend judgment on becoming deeply religious until she saw whether this was typical of the rigors to which she would have to submit. Heavens, what did her destiny have in store for her *next*?

BOOK IV

Fate Gets Dizzy from All Those Savage Turns and Spins

♡　　♡　　♡

Love doth not steal the heart
For love is not a crooke!
—*Richard Milhous, 1817*

Chapter

10

♡   ♡   ♡

*V*anessa's first few days at the convent were a disappointment. To begin with, there was the matter of accommodations. The lushly etched brochure she had been given by Sister Carrie at dockside had breathlessly promised "spacious rms., riv. views, fplc., dbl. beds, rustic charm," but that description hardly concurred with the spartan reality of her new living quarters. Her room, she was saddened to discover, was no more than a whitewashed cell with a spindly double-decker cot and a crucifix on the wall. Worst of all, no drapes had been provided for the small window overlooking the courtyard. If this was what it was like to become a Novice, Vanessa wondered seriously whether she had the faith and stamina needed to become an Intermediate, Advanced, or Pro.

After being given two coarse black robes and a set of that jewelry called rosary beads, Vanessa was brought in to meet the Mother Superior, a large, imposing woman who stood flanked by two other nuns, Mother Erie and Mother Huron.

"Welcome to our place of worship, my child," said the Mother Superior in a firm voice. "Please make thyself comfortable."

By this, the Mother Superior meant that Vanessa should throw herself on the stone floor in abject mortification and abase herself with her arms spread. Given her state of mind, it was just the sort of thing Vanessa hoped to do a lot of, so, concealing her pleasure, Vanessa threw herself to the cold ground, felt deeply mortified, and rose to kiss the Mother Superior's hand.

"Tell me, my child," the Mother Superior inquired kindly, "why hast thou gotten thyself to a nunnery?"

Vanessa smiled confidently. She knew the answer to this one. "To dedicate my life and soul to God the Father, Our Lord Howard."

"Howard?"

"Yes," said Vanessa. "You know, Mother Superior, as in the Lord's Prayer: 'Our Father who art in Heaven, Howard be they name . . . ' "

The Mother Superior cleared her throat. "I think perhaps a bit of remedial catechism is in order," she said. "Thou mayest be off, child."

Vanessa gathered up her robe, which was beginning to be a habit with her, and exited the chamber.

Vanessa walked silently along the corridors of the cloister, thinking of the other disappointments she had had to endure since entering the novitiate: the ungodly hours, the food, the dearth of mirrors—Her meditations were suddenly interrupted by the approach of Shannon, who had just exited the convent's postal office.

"Sister Vanessa," said Shannon, "I have good news!" She then crossed herself before proceeding. Shannon, a deeply pious girl, customarily crossed herself prior to every conversation, sometimes even doing it twice, thereby double-crossing herself.

"I have a letter here from the long-lost cousin of whom I spoke. It has been forwarded to me from my family in Dublin."

"Oh?" said Vanessa. They were walking toward a noisy stream that flowed through the convent's grounds.

"You may recall that I spoke of Bridget when we first arrived here?" Shannon said excitedly. "Well, it seems she went off to New Orleans with her mistress and was left behind on the misty Massahippi—I mean, the mipsy Mippisappi—the . . . "

"Never mind, it's difficult enough for Americans," said Vanessa.

"Yes, well doubtless it means my cousin Bridget is none other than your devoted lady-in-waiting, the so-called Brigitte!"

"Give me that letter that I may read it myself by yon babbling brook," said Vanessa, at last catching on. Taking the letter in her slender, perfect hand she sat on the grass by the talkative stream and began to read.

. . . I thought I should surely perish were it not for the kindness of my new husband, the trapper of mink, otter, and mongoose, Trapper Jacques. When my mistress spurned him, he was so bereft he set fire to the ship in a fit of pique, causing us all to disembark in haste. It was that night, as passengers and crew camped by the banks of the mighty Mississippi, that I prepared for him my *pièce de résistance*— a piece most people resist—otherwise known as potato sherbet. If the route to a man's stomach is indeed through his stomach, as my dear mother in Dublin used to say, it was certainly so with Jacques, although the detour through his liver undoubtedly helped, as I was careful to mix in several bottles of bourbon with the sherbet.

In any case, my Jacques is a reformed man now. He only gambles for money or livestock and has vowed to bathe at least twice a year from now on. At least I think that is what he has sworn, for we communicate through his faithful translator,

Gandhi. Whatever language Trapper Jacques speaks, it is not one I recognize.

And that reminds me—I pray fervently that someday I will find my former mistress, the lady Vanessa, in this wild and savage land. I should like to explain why I felt I had to say I was French in order to gain employment in England after the famine in Ireland because—but hark! I smell my dear Trapper Jacques returning now from the poop deck. I must close now. *Erin go bragh!*

(Dictated to a riverboat scribe, but not read.)

Vanessa put the letter down and stared into the air before her. So Brigitte thought she was Irish! Vanessa knew instinctively that anyone with her lady-in-waiting's cultivation and distinguished accent could no more be Irish than Saint Patrick. Ah well, Vanessa thought tolerantly, it only goes to show. What, she knew not. She only knew that the Lord, whatever his name was, worked in truly hysterical ways.

♡   ♡   ♡

Time passed slowly at the convent, though Vanessa tried to remedy that by shaking her hourglass. Much of the time she spent toiling in the fields of the Lord, and occasionally Vanessa would kick some of the lillies she found growing wild, for they toiled not. Her remedial religious studies were proceeding nicely—my, but the early Christians died in such a variety of ways!—and she even became friendly with her fellow sisters, including Shannon, whom she found to have a kind and generous disposition, for an Irisher.

Nevertheless, she sometimes longed for the restless unpredictability of her life before nunhood. Though her life until then had certainly been tragic, it had not been totally

devoid of laughs. Here at the convent, however, her life was
nothing but pious routines. Is this really how she was destined
to spend the rest of her days, to say nothing of the evenings?
Getting up before dawn; praying; eating a bowl of gruel;
praying; attending high mass; toiling in the fields; then a
change of pace: recreational praying; then some more gruel;
finally, candles out and sleep. This was hardly life on the fast
side of the cobblestones!

Wasn't there *some* respite from this tiresome routine?
Couldn't the sisters occasionally get dressed up in formal
habits and go into town for some dinner and a musical
pageant, or something?

As if her old friend, the celestial spirit, were still hanging
about, Vanessa's entreaties were answered one bright day. At
morning mass, after self-criticism and confession, the Mother
Superior had arisen and announced the news: A week hence
the nuns would be getting together with the monks from a
neighboring monastery, Our Lord of the Sulking Saints. It
was to be the annual Convent-Monastery Coed Picnic! There
would be a holiday atmosphere, including self-flagellation
relay races, a gruel mix-off, and a marathon Hail Mary compe-
tition! It promised to be great fun as well as a deeply moving
religious experience, and Vanessa could hardly wait! Oh joy!
Hialeah!

♡   ♡   ♡

Vanessa had not enjoyed herself so much in a long time.
The sun shone gloriously in the tranquil clearing that had
been chosen for the coed picnic. The air was crisp and
invigorating and all the nuns and monks appeared to be
having great fun, for which they all would of course have to

sincerely repent later that evening. Vanessa situated herself upon a flat rock in the shade to observe the many activities. Over yonder was Shannon, participating in a potato-sack race with several Irish monks; across the sylvan glade were two teams playing badminton, today renamed goodminton as it was being played in the service of the Lord. Even the Mother Superior seemed to be enjoying herself in a wrestling match with the stout and muscular Abbot of the monastery.

But it was a game called cricket that seemed most interesting to Vanessa. The game was still in its primitive stages, to be sure, as its rules seemed to consist of players tramping through the underbrush, swatting crickets and other hopping insects with wooden bats. When enough crickets had been swatted in this manner, the players were said to have "sticky wickets." It was a puzzling game, not the least reason being that the monks who were playing it were doing so in complete silence.

"They are Trappists," Shannon explained earlier. Vanessa had flinched, thinking of an encounter with a trapper upon the mighty Mississippi. But Shannon assuaged her fears, explaining that Trappists were a fraternal order of monks who had taken vows of silence.

"They cannot speak?" Vanessa had asked. "Then how do they communicate?"

"Watch," said Shannon.

And indeed, as a fraternal dispute arose over the swatting of a cricket, Vanessa noticed that one monk went up to a monk who was acting as referee and angrily kicked dirt over the referee's sandals. There followed an elaborate ritual of hand signals between the two monks, consisting of fingers to signify words and syllables, and mime to act out words and ideas. When one of the monks had caught on to what was being mimed, the signaler placed a finger on his nose to signify that he had it. What an odd way to say things!

Suddenly her attention was caught by the sight of an older monk engaged in the cricket game. He was in his fifties, with steel-grey hair and penetrating green eyes of the purest azure. He was quite dashing, piously speaking, even with the bald spot upon his head. But the oddest thing was his undeniable resemblance to Vanessa: the same firm chin, the same high cheekbones, the same flawless complexion. It was almost as if she were holding up a long-forgotten mirror and were beholding herself in his face. She wondered how that could be and drifted into a reverie as the cricket game continued.

Then an unusual thing occurred. The handsome older monk had bent over to swat a cricket when an enormous bee stung him upon his posterior, right through the fabric of his robe! Obviously pained by the sudden sting, he mouthed a silent cry and gripped his backside, falling down in agony.

The game came to a halt as the monk's teammates made the sign of the T to the referee, and the Abbot rushed over to see what was the matter. The Abbot was not bound by vows of silence.

"What has befallen thee, Brother Al?" he asked the fallen monk.

Brother Al, still writhing upon the ground, used his unusual sign language.

"One syllable," the Abbot said. "You're on a . . . sofa! No? A . . . bed! A couch! *Sounds* like a couch? Shorter? Shorter than a couch? Ouch! Is it Ouch?"

Brother Al was holding his finger to his nose, nodding his head vigorously.

"Lift thy cassock that I may see wherefore thou sayest Ouch," intoned the Abbot. Most of the nuns looked piously away, but Vanessa, whose restless nature made her curious, watched the comical scene. As the Abbot bared the handsome monk's backside, she saw first the swollen welt from the bee sting. But then she saw something that made her gasp and caused her heart to hammer. It was the rash!

Indeed, there, in the afternoon sun, on the posterior of a monk she had never met, was a rose-colored heart-shaped rash! It was absolutely identical to hers! What could this mean?

She was about to rush forward and interrogate the monk when she looked over and saw the Mother Superior staring sternly at her. Apparently thinking Vanessa was watching the scene with impure thoughts, the presiding nun walked firmly over to Vanessa and said, "Thou shouldst cast away thine gaze, Sister Vanessa!" When Vanessa looked away, momentarily embarrassed, the Mother Superior softened. "It is all right, my child, we all have lapses. When thou returnest to the convent this evening, thou shouldst say five hundred Hail Marys and two thousand Our Fathers in atonement."

Vanessa nodded in compliance, though the fiery, stubborn part of her nature remained determined to question the monk about the rash at the earliest convenience. What *could* the reckless stigma, first seen on her thigh, now on his posterior, signify?

As Brother Al was attended by the Abbot, his signals of pain gently subsiding, Vanessa sat by the babbling brook in contemplation, attempting to make some sense out of this odd coincidence. Then suddenly she recalled the episode aboard the H.M.S. *Freddie*, when Gypsy Rose Leigh reacted to seeing the heart-shaped rash on Vanessa's thigh. What was it Rose Leigh had said about the last time she had seen such a rash?

"It was on the backside . . . of an English monk . . . in Sussex named . . . Brother Al," the Gypsy had said. Vanessa repeated the key words over and over: "On the backside . . . of Brother Al . . . On the backside . . . of Brother Al . . ."

Could it be? Could there be a similarity between the Brother Al that the Gypsy told her about, the one with a heart-shaped rash on his backside who lived in Sussex, and the Brother Al she had just seen here in Sussex, with a heart-shaped rash on *his* backside? Could they be related? A canny suspicion occurred to her: Aha! They couldn't be one and the same, could they?

Furthermore, hadn't Rose Leigh implied that there was some guilty secret linked to that rash? Could this tie in somehow to the fact that her departed One True Love was supposed to be her brother? Could it have something to do with the guilty secret her mother went to her grave with? Could we be reaching some kind of plot climax here? A gentle swoon of breathless realization swept through her, causing her to sway gently upon her rocky perch. How wonderfully filled with coincidences, she thought, was the life of a romantic heroine!

Presently the afternoon's amusements resumed, as the nuns and monks gathered for a picnic of fish and loaves. Brother Al, she could see from the corner of her eye, had retired his poor posterior to a mossy spot beneath a tree. His pain appeared to have subsided, and as the Mother Superior and the Abbot were occupied attempting to multiply the fish and loaves, Vanessa walked inconspicuously over to where Brother Al sat.

He looked up at her curiously as she approached, and for a moment it seemed to Vanessa as if a painful recognition flashed upon his features. It vanished quickly, however, and Vanessa wondered for a few seconds how she should question him. She decided he would respond best if she used the *thees*, *thys*, and *thous* she had been practicing nightly in her cell. Yet she struggled within herself to find a way to begin her interrogation in a subtle, discreet way.

"Doth the name Sherwin-Williams ring a bell?" she inquired of the monk.

As if struck by a holy ax handle, Brother Al looked stunned. He jumped up to his feet with a look of fear contorting his handsome features and strode away without a single hand signal.

"Hold thy horses!" Vanessa cried, for she had determined that, one way or the other, she would get to the bottom—so to speak—of the mystery of her reckless rash. But the monk failed to halt his figurative steeds and, indeed, began to run into the woods as fast as his sandals would carry him. Vanessa hitched up her habit and began to run after him. Their scramble attracted the attention of two nuns nearby, Sister Ingrid, who had recently been transferred from a Bavarian convent, and Sister Cynthia, a pious Scotswoman. Both were exceptionally voluptuous nuns.

"Oh, goodie!" said Sister Cynthia excitedly, "a footrace! I'll bet two rosaries on Sister Vanessa in the first!" Sister Cynthia was actually known as Sister Thia, for such was her piety that she had chosen to be without Cyn.

"You will lose zat bet!" exclaimed Sister Ingrid, slapping her beads down in acceptance. Sister Ingrid was a fiery sort, often in trouble with her superiors for her habit of wearing her habit somewhat low-cut.

But momentarily the runners were out of sight and deep into the woods.

♡   ♡   ♡

As the chase ensued, Brother Al and Sister Vanessa went farther and farther into a thick forest consisting principally of trees. As Brother Al was middle-aged, and Vanessa young and stubbornly determined, she soon caught up with him and tackled him demurely by pinning him to the ground and sitting upon him.

"And now, the truth!" she exclaimed, catching her breath. "I must know, Brother Al! I have a birthrash identical to thine! Art thou—oh, drat the thous!—are you related to me?"

The monk nodded.

"Am I related to you?"

The monk nodded again, a bit impatiently.

"Are we related to each other?"

The monk nodded exasperatedly.

"Then. . .could . . . you be . . . my . . . father?"

The monk, who had been struggling beneath her, suddenly became still. A tear welled up in one eye, then the other. Slowly, sadly, he reached up and put a finger to his nose—she'd gotten it—and nodded his head.

Vanessa arose from her newfound relative's chest, took a few steps away, and threw herself upon the ground, never being one to let a potentionally melodramatic moment pass her by. Holding her face in her hands, she wept as the floodwaters of the tidal wave of tears cascaded down her flawless cheeks.

Moments later she attempted to compose herself while she awaited Brother Al's silent explanation.

Vanessa asked, "What are you prepared to tell me?"

Brother Al signaled with his thumb and forefinger, indicating something small.

"Small word?" guessed Vanessa. "The?" Brother Al nodded and signaled for the second word. "Second word . . .

sounds like . . . uncouth? . . . forsooth? . . . truth? The
Truth!"

And so Vanessa sat down to watch the whole story
unfold, apprehensive but happy that the truth would at last
come out. It was bound to be complicated, especially given
the silent language the monk was forced to use. But how long
could it take to find out the simple truth? she thought.

Eighteen hours later, as dawn broke through the trees,
Vanessa had her explanation. So exhausted was she that she
did not know immediately whether to be grieved or stricken.
But just to be sure that she had the story correctly, she
repeated the entire explanation back to the monk, who had
become tired and irritable, and had a cramp in his fingers.

"Just to make sure I have it correctly, we'll go over it
once more, all right?" she asked. Brother Al nodded wearily.

"According to what you have just signaled me," she
began, "some twenty years ago, being of noble birth and high
standing at court, you were on a fox hunt in Devonshire. You
had been drinking heavily with your noble companions, and
wishing to find some more distilled spirits, you came upon a
castle and began pounding upon the door. Correct so far?"
Brother Al nodded guiltily.

"A beautiful woman came to the door, and as her husband was away, you recklessly demanded some grog. When
she told you she had none, you pushed your way in, and, your
senses inflamed by this woman's beauty, you . . . had your
way with her. Is that also correct?" The monk's chin was deep
into his neck as he nodded in shame.

"After returning home and becoming sober, you made
inquiries and found out the woman whose Person you had
violated was Lady Sherwin-Williams. What your investiga-
tions also told you was that although she was married to Lord
Sherwin-Williams, she had for years been conducting a passionate friendship with the Duke of Earl, Senior. He was the

man she *should* have married, but that's another romantic story, correct?"

Another nod.

"So there was a deep romantic feeling between them, but as faithfully married persons, they were strictly intimate with each other's mind and nothing south of there, correct?"

Brother Al nodded sheepishly.

"Sometime later you found out that Lady Sherwin-Williams was expecting a child. She then delivered an exquisitely beautiful baby girl whose eyes were a topaz the color of yellow sapphires. The baby was named Vanessa. But because Lord Sherwin-Williams had been away for ten months and would thus suspect something was amiss, the gallant Duke of Earl offered to announce that *he* was the father, and that I, Vanessa, was the offspring of their adulterous union. But once he had done this, they were so distraught at no longer being able to see each other because of the scandal, and at having to break off their platonic, but passionate, friendship . . . they both committed suicide together!" Vanessa was sobbing now. "Am I right so far?"

Another weary nod.

"And so, out of remorse for your drunken action and the consequences that followed, you disappeared from the county and joined the clergy, taking a vow of silence and deciding to spend the rest of your days in a monastery, correct?"

So ended the tragic tale—long, tedious, heartbreaking, and incredibly contrived.

Vanessa could only whisper now.

"Then . . . the young Duke of Earl was never my sibling, was he?"

Brother Al, as a change of pace, shook his weary head.

Vanessa, choking, felt tears of pity and forgiveness well up in her eyes.

"Then you are truly my beloved father, Brother!"

"And you are truly my beloved daughter, Sister!" he signaled back.

And the two embraced and wept in each other's arms, one silently and the other noisily, as they knelt upon the moss of the sylvan forest, alone save for the birds, the insects, the rodents, and several hundred other varieties of wildlife.

Vanessa could not help herself from wondering: What now of her destiny?

Chapter

♡   ♡   ♡

Taking her farewell of the convent had been both sad and joyous. Since there was no longer any need for her to be cloistered, she was given a dispensation and her vows were annulled. And though devoting herself to God had provided her with great solace in her time of need, it had certainly not been rife with romantic possibilities. And so she bade good-bye to the Mother Superior, and to Mothers Huron and Erie, and even to the nun who had recruited her with somewhat misleading promises, Sister Carrie. Then she tearfully embraced her friend Shannon, as well as the other nun-friends she had made—Mother Marianne, Mother Beverly, Sister Michele, Sister Stephanie, Sister Minkie—there were so many of them!

Clad in her habit, as it was all she had, she walked three miles into the nearest village, where she inquired about a rent-a-steed firm owned by a tradesman named Hertz. He informed her that a domestic steed would cost her ten shillings a day, whereas a noble Arabian steed would cost more. Vanessa, ever a woman of taste, chose the Arabian.

Shortly thereafter, she was galloping down the highway that led away from the convent as if her heart had taken flight. With her habit and veil fluttering in the wind, she knew she must resemble some sort of flying nun, an image she found ludicrous in the extreme. Yes, she would miss her friends of the cloth, but after Brother Al's tumultuous revelations, she knew that she must flee the world of black robes and vespers and silences and unseemly hairdos. She was free at last!

Although her One True Love was tragically defunct, at least she no longer suffered the guilt of having been in love with her brother, as she had thought for so long. Since she and the departed young Duke of Earl were unrelated, it lifted the burden from her shoulders, which were slender, small-boned, and white-skinned. However, what to do next was the big question. She knew only that she had a nostalgic desire to visit her homestead, the imposing Sherwin-Williams Castle, and see what changes had occurred there since her adventures abroad.

The midafternoon shadows were beginning to spread across the highway as she urged her faithful Arabian steed down an empty, lonely stretch. The woods on either side were lovely, dark, and deep and the gait of her steed was lulling her to sleep, but the Frost in the air kept her awake.

Suddenly he was in front of her. Out of nowhere, she saw him sitting astride a magnificent white stallion. He was blocking any progress along the highway, his face in a threatening black mask, a long, shiny pistol pointed at her Person. From various clues, she shrewdly guessed he was a Highwayman. It was apparent that he was handsome beneath the mask, and tall, very tall. He wore a shirt that opened at the top to reveal curly dark chest hair, and he had a bright red belt that both accented his wardrobe and held up his pants. If this man were not a desperate criminal on the point of committing unspeakable felonies, Vanessa thought, he just might be capable of making a fashion statement.

She pulled on the reins to bring her steed to a complete halt. As she drew closer, her veil blew across the exquisite features of her face, thus obscuring them. The masked Highwayman lowered his pistol. Vanessa realized at once she was safe, that the Highwayman, criminal that he was, nevertheless had enough fear of the Lord and respect for the cloth not to hold her up. He might be a lot of things, but he did not mug nuns.

His voice, when he finally spoke, was resonant and profoundly virile.

"I beg your pardon, Sister," said the Highwayman, holding the reins taut as his magnificent stallion stomped the ground. It was obvious that he, too, had a proud Arabian steed, and that his Arabian steed did not care for *her* Arabian steed. Perhaps Arabs just didn't get along, Vanessa thought. The Highwayman continued: "I would not keep you from your mission for the Lord. My quarrel is only with the rich and powerful, the oppressors who come this way. I relieve them of surplus riches and distribute them among the poor."

If there was one thing Vanessa was *not* in the mood for, it was politics.

"You should be ashamed of yourself, nonetheless, sirrah!" she exclaimed. "What you do is illegal, illicit, immoral, and . . . ill-advised!" She was rather pleased at this last turn of phrase. Something in this scoundrel was bringing out her gift for repartee.

"No, Good Sister," said the Highwayman, putting away his pistol. "Circumstances have forced me into this way of life. If you knew my tragic past, you would have Christian pity for my lot."

Vanessa was not moved. *"Your* tragic past? Sir, tragedy and Lost Love are as brother and sister to me—and *I* have not fallen into a life of crime!" She tried to keep the veil out of her face, which kept obscuring her flawless features. "No, it is clear that you are thoroughly bad—a scoundrel, a rake and a—a—hoe!"

The Highwayman rocked back in his saddle as if he had been run through by a Bengal lance. His head snapped, his shoulders came forward, and his knees jerked upward. Something was evidently concerning him.

"What did you just call me, Good Sister?" he asked, choking on his words. As soon as he had coughed them up, he resumed his incredulity. "Did you happen to call me a . . . hoe?"

"Why, yes," Vanessa said, blushing deeply. As if stirred by a celestial spirit, the wind died down, the veil fell away from her exquisite face, and this time the Highwayman let out an audible but virile gasp. His entire body was once again rocked back in the saddle. It occurred to Vanessa that this particular Highwayman might need a brush-up lesson in equestrian stability.

"It cannot be!" thundered the Highwayman. He suddenly swung a muscled leg over the rump of his Arabian steed and jumped to the ground. "Can it possibly be?" he shouted, running toward Vanessa. "By all that is precious in this world of fleeting goodness, can it be?" Vanessa had only time to reflect that though he was a wordy Highwayman, he was her sort of wordsman. Suddeny he was by her side.

"Vanessa!" he cried, reaching up for her. "Vanessa! It is I, your One True Love!" She looked down at him, deeply puzzled. As she was sitting sidesaddle, it was easy for him to suddenly take her by the waist and pull her down into his waiting arms. Before she knew what has happening, she was resisting him, pushing at him, pounding her small but perfect fists against his massive, lightly hairy chest.

"Get away from me!" she shouted, resisting him with a certain amount of her strength. "Let me down, you brute, you beast!" She was breathing heavily as the Highwayman picked her up in his manly arms, and she pounded at his chest some more. "You cad!" she cried. "My One True Love is dead, deeply dead, and you have no right to call yourself by that name!"

Suddenly, surprisingly, inappropriately, the Highwayman lifted his head to the sky as he tightened his masculine grip on her and . . . laughed! It was a deep-throated, full-bodied laugh that sounded at once thrilling, reassuring—and familiar! Could it . . . might it . . . ? Oh, no, it couldn't. . . . The dots were upon her, for the first time in these many months. This was some terrible . . . dream. . . . It had to be. . . . It was the . . . only . . . explanation!

As if reading her jumbled thoughts, the Highwayman paused in his resonant laughter and, using the hand that held her firmly beneath the shoulders, suddenly reached up and . . . whipped away his mask!

It was he!

It was the Duke of Earl!

It was her beloved Anthony, as alive and whole and dry as the last precious second they had spent together!

That was all she had time to allow into her brain, for she was falling, falling into—at last!—an industrial-strength, pull-out-the-stopper, indisputable swoon! And just before the world went dark, she knew that she was looking into the piercing grey eyes of her One True Love and that now, after all of her travails, she could allow herself to faint. Finally, mercifully, she passed out.

Although she was sure she had fallen into an all-out swoon, the truth was that in the excitement of the moment, when the handsome young Duke of Earl had used his hand to whip away his Highwayman mask, he had left the upper part of Vanessa's nearly flawless body unsupported. She had thus fallen on her head and been knocked unconscious.

Nevertheless, as she awoke, she found that her head was

cradled in the young Duke's arms. He was sitting upon the ground, stroking her hair, rubbing the bump upon her otherwise perfect head, whispering sweet somethings to her. Meanwhile, the two Arabian steeds muttered at each other, snorting menacingly.

"Oh, oh, please wake up, my little buttercup," whispered the Duke.

She fluttered her long, slender eyelashes.

"And what if I do not, my large hyacinth?"

The stroking stopped. He realized with a start that she was fully conscious and his face broke out in a heavenly smile.

"Then I shall have to wake you with love, my precious sneezeweed," he said, brushing her hair back. Oh, God, it was true-blue, genuine romance again, complete with horticultural banter! She did not for the moment question how it had come to pass, but the chase was on again!

"Then perhaps I will indeed hasten to awaken, my huge philodendron!" she exclaimed teasingly.

"Is that so, my shade-tolerant hydrangea?"

At this they both felt aroused, and as if released from the constraints of death and beyond, as if the tempests of titanic love had loosed upon them a squall of the most phlegmatic emotional moisture, he leaned down, gripped her chin in his finely knuckled hands, and kissed her deeply. It was the same searing kiss she remembered from the night in the garden so many months ago; the same fiery buss she remembered from her countless dreams of passion. It was he, and she was she and they were they. Everything was in its place, including the pronouns, and she knew not nor cared not how it had come to be! Somehow, on this lonely stretch of road, she had come face-to-mask with the one person in this world who could have made her want to love and live—and he was supposed to have been dead!

Which reminded her.

"How—how—how come you to be here, my love?" she asked, coming up for air. "Your poor body was supposed to have been crushed to a pulp 'neath the Cliffs of Rover!"

He, too, paused in his searing kisses.

"It is a long story, my love," he said. "But suffice it to say that the peasant woman who reported my fall had been a faithful family retainer of mine since I was a mere stripling." Vanessa gasped. "Yes, she lied and said I had fallen—or jumped—and that my body was carried out to sea."

"And the truth?" asked Vanessa, biting her lips in anticipation.

"The truth is that I was profoundly bereft for a fortnight after you left, knowing that because we were brother and sister, we could never consummate our True Love," he explained, brimming over with sincerity. "Then, when I fatally wounded Lord Gastleigh in the head, I knew I must give up my life of pleasures. Yes, Vanessa, until I met you my life had consisted of two things: fighting or attending dances—dueling or balling, in other words.

"Without you to hope for, with the Devonshire authorities after me for the death of Lord Gastleigh, I felt I had only two choices as a gentleman: suicide or a life of crime."

"And which did you choose?" she asked.

"As might be apparent, I chose to become a Highwayman and thus pay my debt to society. And"—he suddenly became grave—"to forget you!" As if suddenly remembering what he had forgotten, he put his hands to his face as if to weep.

Vanessa sat up.

"What is it, my darling?" she asked.

"In that respect—forgetting you—nothing has changed!" he cried out in agony. "You are my sister and I dare not speak what our love must be!" He wept large, masculine tears.

It was such a precious, adorable misunderstanding, and he looked so cute and romantic with the tears streaming down his face that Vanessa was tempted to prolong it. After all, how many occassions in a lifetime did a gal get in a situation like *this?*

But presently she could no longer bear the Duke's true agony and she decided to tell him the whole truth.

"Oh, Anthony," she said, reaching over to wipe away his tears with her long, silken hair. Then she remembered they had bobbed it in the convent and used the hem of her habit. "Oh, Anthony, you poor, dear fool! Do you not know that Lord Gastleigh is not dead at all?" The Duke slowed down the rate of his manly sobs. "That is right," she continued. "You merely wounded him!" The young Duke looked grateful for this, but he was obviously awaiting the more significant news.

"And as for our being brother and sister," she continued happily, "that is a complete fabrication!" And she proceeded to relate the story surrounding her reckless rash.

At this, a suddenly dry-eyed Duke of Earl leapt to his feet, uttered a cry of joy, and pulled her up to him. His mouth hungrily sought hers, giving her the sort of searing kiss she had long dreamed of, their bodies uniting as if they were one, or, at most, two. This was it. The long wait was over. They were free to love, free to live, free to be to each other what they were intended by Fate to be. At this realization, and as his body pushed more insistently but lovingly against her, she could feel in her body the evidence that she had finally achieved what she had set out to find—one hundred percent, simultaneous rapture. The Big R was hers at last!

♡   ♡   ♡

The return to Sherwin-Williams Castle was accomplished swiftly. Walking together into the Great Parlour, they found that

the kindly old Duke's condition had deteriorated. His doctors
had been treating him for symptoms of advanced looniness, and
he was only partly in remission. He, who had so forcefully exiled
Vanessa, who had spent a good part of his life convinced she was
the bastard child of his wife and the senior Duke of Earl,
accepted Vanessa's summary of the real facts meekly and mildly.
He nodded as she made her points, once or twice glancing at the
young Duke of Earl sheepishly.

"And so, dear Papa, you see that you have accused my
beloved mother of dallying with the wrong man. It was not with
the elder Duke of Earl at all! Anthony and I are free to love each
other! Are you not happy for us?"

In way of reply, the kindly old Duke took out his family
scepter and gave his head a smart *thwack!* Heavens, it was good
to be back!

Adopting a serious mien, the young Duke stepped forward
to address Vanessa's adoptive father.

"M'lord, I have a matter of the gravest concern to raise with
you. May I have your attention?"

The kindly old Duke paused in his pastime and looked
curiously at the young man.

"M'lord," he continued, "I have the honor to ask you for
the hand of your daughter."

There was a pause.

"Is that all?" asked the kindly old Duke.

"Beg pardon, m'lord?" Anthony was caught off balance.

"Her hand, fine. What of her foot?"

"Well—" stammered the young Duke. "All right. That,
too. I have the honor of asking you for the hand *and* foot of your
daughter. May I have your response, sir?"

"What about her torso?"

Anthony flashed a despairing look at Vanessa, who could
only shrug her adorable shoulders. There was nothing to be
done, they both realized, but go through the entire catalogue of

anatomical features until the kindly old Duke was convinced Anthony meant to propose to *all* of her.

Forty minutes later, Anthony was at the limits of his knowledge of body language.

" . . . May I also have the honor of asking you for the pancreas of your daughter, m'lord?" At that moment, the kindly old Duke dozed off, scepter in his hand and a happy, nodding smile on his face. The lovers embraced, knowing the way was at long last clear.

♡   ♡   ♡

The wedding itself was the event of the county social season. The Archbishop of Devonshire presided in the Devonshire Abbey, with all the important people of the district in attendance. Earls and Viscounts and Princes of the realm occupied the most important pews, and even the Duchess of Winston, she of the large balls, attended the nuptials.

There was Vanessa's adoptive father, of course, the kindly old Duke, who thoroughly approved the union now, but was somewhat vague about where he was. After being wheeled into the first pew, he would alternate between kneeling at the appropriate moments of the solemn high mass and jumping to his feet to cheer the Oxford crew to victory. Then there were Vanessa's stepsisters, who came in somewhat less charitable moods than their father. Lady Gertrude scowled at everybody, Lady Agnes decked a solicitous flower girl with a hard right, and Lady Ralph physically occupied most of one pew by herself.

The biggest surprise came just before the service when Vanessa, breathtaking in a gown of purest white, thought she sniffed a familiar odor wafting in from outside the abbey. It brought back certain memories, some of them less than pleasant, but nonetheless linked to her romantic past. As she turned her flawless head, which swiveled perfectly on a slender, swanlike neck, she caught sight of—Trapper Jacques! Yes, it was the reeking French fur trapper, come all the way from the mighty Mississippi to attend this event. And of even greater joy to Vanessa was the sight of the woman on Trapper Jacques's arm: It was her beloved French lady-in-waiting, Brigitte! They made their own quaint procession up the aisle, causing chuchgoers on Trapper Jacques's side to keel over from the fumes. To complete the pretty picture, Gandhi was also there, faithful to the last.

But the most heartwarming surprise was that Lord Gastleigh had also decided to attend, apparently willing to forgive Anthony for having created his handicap. In fact, before the ceremony, Anthony had put his arm around the young Lord and said, "You know, Gastleigh, this could be the beginning of a beautiful friendship," at which everybody in earshot, including Vanessa, had wept. For his part, Gastleigh had grinned imbecilically. Now Gastleigh stood at the back of the church, his dueling sword still swinging like a pendulum, acting as metronome for the church organist.

Everyone agreed that the ceremony was the longest in the memory of the county. When the Archbishop of Devonshire finished his homily he directed that the congregation be awakened by a couple of loud blasts of the organ. As for the bride and groom—Vanessa was so heart-stopping that several elderly gentlemen held up their hymn books in front of their eyes as she passed, and Anthony was as always resplendently handsome in a formal black cutaway and top hat, his ruffled white shirt cut low so his manly chest hair showed off to advantage.

Suddenly, they had been pronounced man and wife and were walking down the aisle and out the huge oaken doors of the abbey. The bells of the abbey began to peal, then the bells in the other churches of the county followed suit with merry pealing, until much of Devonshire was littered with rinds. In harmony with the church bells, Lord Gastleigh gonged the hours melodiously. It was a beautiful Spring day, the kind of day that could last a Person a lifetime, thought Vanessa.

As they came down the abbey steps together, hand in flawless hand, the young Duke bent down, held her chin, and gave the new Duchess of Earl a warm, gratifying, and comfortable kiss upon her full, lush, supple, ruby-red, heart-shaped lips.

Vanessa paused to savor the effect. Hmmmm, she thought. It was a good kiss. It was a loving kiss. But was it . . . a . . . passionate kiss? More precisely, was it as passionate a kiss now that they were married as it had been before?

This was a whole new romantic dilemma.

Of course, they would live happily ever after, Vanessa knew instinctively. It was just that men will be men, even if they happen to be a Person's One True Love. She was going to have to watch for those teensy signs that suggested an ebbing of ardor. After all, she reflected as they walked eastward into the sunset, was that not her destiny? To be vigilant that standards were being upheld? Else why was a romantic heroine put upon this Earth?

The End